I0816262

The Way Home is rich, accessible theology for real disciples. Graham Shearer lifts our eyes to the glory of the Christian journey—rooted in the gospel, sustained by grace, and headed toward glory—guiding us to the finish line with clarity and warmth. This is the kind of book that helps churches and believers keep going—and to keep going with joy.

Nate Akin
Executive Director, Pillar Network

I love the laser-like focus of *The Way Home.* In just about every paragraph Graham Shearer pinpoints the battles, blindspots and blessings for the Christian journey I'm on. I wholeheartedly recommend it to any fellow traveller.

Rico Tice
Christianity Explored

This is a wise, warm, and wonderfully down-to-earth companion for weary travelers on the road to glory. With honesty, humor, and gospel clarity, it reminds us that the Christian life is not aimless wandering but a purposeful journey with Jesus—the Way, the Truth, and the Life. Whether you are just setting out, feeling lost, or tempted to give up, these pages will steady your steps and lift your eyes to the destination that makes every struggle worth it.

Paul Rees
Lead Pastor, Charlotte Chapel, Edinburgh

We often face our hardest struggles when we lack a clear picture of how difficulties can bring bright conclusions. That's especially true in the Christian life when sin habits, Satan's devices, and personal weakness dull us, and worse, attempt to wrench us from faithfulness to Christ. With pastoral gentleness, Graham Shearer shepherds readers with a full picture of Jesus Christ's saving and keeping power for every believer in his new book, *The Way Home.* His clarity, winsomeness, and honesty weaves a trustworthy story of the Christian's life and how the Christian can keep pressing on with reliance upon the Lord Jesus. While Graham told his story, so often I thought I was reading my own. I found his encouragement toward endurance in the Christian life to be a balm for my soul. This is a book you'll want to read, savor, and give copies to friends to encourage them in the journey of following Jesus from now to eternity.

Phil A. Newton
Director of Pastoral Care & Mentoring, Pillar Network;
Author, *Unburdening the Soul: Personal and Corporate Confession of Sin*

Some books instruct while others inspire, but this one walks with you. Graham is a friend and colleague I've come to know as deeply pastoral and relational, and those same qualities shape every page. He doesn't write as a distant guide but as a fellow traveller on the way home. He's honest about the challenges and eager to encourage weary saints to keep going. With his characteristic warmth and clarity, he brings the great truths of Scripture down to where real life is lived. Whether you are just starting out, stumbling along, or straining toward the finish, you'll find in these pages encouragement, clarity, and hope.

Matthew Marshall
Pastor, Glenrothes Baptist Church

The Way Home carries the unmistakable scent of a shepherd's heart, shaped by years of faithfully loving both his family and his church family in Scotland. This is not theory; it is wisdom forged in the fires of real pastoral life. Whether you're just setting out on the Christian journey, or finding yourself weary along the way, this book offers direction, comfort, and a steady hand to guide you forward. It will speak to the seeker and to the seasoned saint. Indeed, I found myself deeply encouraged by its reminder that the Lord will indeed carry His children all the way home. I commend this book most highly to all.

Jonathan E. McClaughlin

Principal, Irish Baptist College; Pastor, Hamilton Road Baptist Church, Bangor, Northern Ireland

The Way Home is an excellent introduction to the Christian life. Graham Shearer explains the gospel and its implications in a manner that is both clear and compelling. This book will encourage those who already follow Christ, as an aid to discipleship. It will help those who have questions and hesitations, showing the goodness and beauty of submitting to the truth. I pray *The Way Home* will help many follow Jesus unto glory.

Paul Twiss

Teaching Pastor, Bethany Bible Church, Thousand Oaks, California

Every great journey needs a trustworthy guide, a faithful companion, and a worthwhile destination. In this wise and uplifting book, Graham Shearer shows us that Jesus is all of these and infinitely more besides. Whether you are just starting out or have been traveling for years, this book will help you begin well, stay the course, and keep going with hope. It reminds us that every step and every struggle is worth it, because what lies ahead is far better than anything left behind.

Jon Gemmell
Director, Cornhill Training Course, Glasgow

The people around us each day seem to move through life with little purpose. Aimless. Directionless. One day to the next with little intentionality or mission. It's no wonder that it's hard for many to get out of bed each morning when there's not much to live for. *The Way Home* provides a compelling portrayal of a gospel-motivated, Christ-exalting, heaven-directed purpose for human existence. Read it and find yourself pulled forward into each new day with hope that God is at work through the journey of your life to bring you safely home.

Matt Rogers
Resourcing and Fundraising Coordinator, Pillar Network

These warm and encouraging words come from the heart of someone deeply rooted in pastoral experience. This book will help you keep moving forward in your Christian journey, written by one who genuinely loves to guide and support others.

Andrew Curry
Senior Pastor, Trinity Bible Church, Dallas, Texas

THE WAY HOME

Following Jesus from Now to Eternity

Graham Shearer

paperback ISBN 978-1-5271-1317-6
ebook ISBN 978-1-5271-1405-0

Published in 2026 by
Christian Focus Publications Ltd,
Geanies House, Fearn, Ross-shire,
IV20 1TW, Great Britain.
www.christianfocus.com

Cover design by Simon Oliver

Printed and bound by Bell and Bain, Glasgow

In memory of Mark Beattie, my friend and brother in Christ, who showed me what true contentment in Jesus means.

Contents

Foreword

Ben Macdui is the second highest mountain in the United Kingdom. It is known for its challenging but rewarding hiking routes. Finding a way to the summit is difficult on account of the lack of distinct landmarks especially when the fog rolls in. The travel brochures suggest a number of potential starting places and hikers are 'encouraged' to prepare for potentially harsh weather, including biting winds. It would be unwise to attempt the journey alone. Fortunately for me I was not alone when as a young teenager I set out in the company of older experienced guides who knew the way. Such is the journey of the Christian life – often described as a long obedience in the one direction. It might equally be referred to as the ascent – the Hebrew word "aliyah" meaning ascent or rise – described the people of God going up to Jerusalem. That the pilgrimage was not made alone is clear in the words of the Psalmist: "I was glad when they said to me let us go up to the house of the Lord". The same leaders who served as my guides also taught me to sing:

> There's a grand highway
> That is free to all
> And it leads to the King's abode.
> It starts at the cross where Jesus died
> It is there we must join the road.

If setting out at the correct place is vital, it is equally important that we continue along the way in the right direction. For some of us the middle part of the journey may prove to be the toughest. This is not an unusual experience in seeking to press on towards the goal as we look to Jesus.

Our author has provided us with a wonderfully Biblical and practical guide to help us face the challenges along the way by reminding us that "He who began a good work in us will bring it to completion at the day of Jesus Christ". The importance of this cannot be overestimated because we can never lead souls heavenward unless climbing ourselves, we need not be very high up, but we must be climbing.

So whether you find yourself in the position of Thomas who asked "how can we know the way?" or you are struggling to keep going, I commend this book to you as one who throughout my life has been profoundly helped along The Way by the author's father, John, and now by the author himself.

Alistair Begg
Truth For Life
Chagrin Falls, Ohio

Acknowledgements

Being on The Way is meant to be a relational experience and by God's grace it has been for me. I cannot imagine what travelling solo to Heaven would look like, but I am thankful I don't need to. This book was birthed during a sabbatical that my loving church in Musselburgh afforded to me. I am grateful to all of the leaders and members for your care of our family and for choosing to listen to me as I seek to feed you with the Scriptures. I love you all.

Although 50 years old I am still a son, and my parents continue to be precious gifts that Heaven has sent my way. Mum and Dad, you show me what journeying to the New World looks like. Keep going to the very end. Our whole family is forever grateful for you both!

Shona, one of our members, and Anne were my editors, and I am indebted to both for their patience as they worked through thc tcxt.

In many respects I wrote this book for our children. Hannah, Ethan, Abigail, Caleb, Esther and Mila – you are all precious. The Lord made you and He did that so you would love Him for all of your days. My relentless prayer, along with your mum, is that you would treasure Christ above all things. Every other shrine promises the world, but the world is no match for Jesus.

Lastly, the super-hero in our family and my faithful ever-present travelling companion. Being on The Way with you, Sarah, has involved lots of twists and turns in the road but your love for Jesus, our children, and me has never wavered. 'The boundary lines have fallen for me in pleasant places.' I love journeying with you.

Introduction

This is a mercifully short(ish) book about a long journey with God. So long that its length and scope is captured perfectly by that great theologian of our day, Buzz Lightyear, when he speaks of going 'to infinity and beyond'.[1] It is a father/child epic adventure that starts at a specific point, continues on a specific route, and then culminates at a specific destination, a destination that will be more glorious than all the other places put together that we have journeyed to in this world.

Moreover, Jesus has pledged that we will make it to the end. He once said that 'I give them (His sheep) eternal life and they shall *never* perish' (John 10:28).[2] I can't describe how comforting that is to me! Friends of ours have just popped by on their way to the Serengeti for their honeymoon. It will be truly spectacular – but not a patch on where Christians are going. An unspoiled and unending Heaven. And in the end it will be worth every step, every tear, and every ounce of perspiration that has dripped from our spiritual pores. We may doubt that at

1 Buzz Lightyear is one of the main characters in the Disney – Pixar Toy Story franchise.

2 As noted by J.C. Ryle there is a transition in John 10 from the character of Christ's sheep to the privileges that they receive. "He gives to them eternal life; the precious gift of pardon and grace in this world, and a life of glory in the world to come.' J.C. Ryle, *John* Vol 2, Expository Thoughts on the Gospels (Edinburgh: Banner of Truth Trust, 2012), 128.

times in the hard seasons, but those questions will be forever silenced when our journey ends and faith gives way to sight. We will be there. Joy uncontained!

Undoubtedly, along the way there will be moments that we will wish to bottle and keep as our fuel for the road – times of immense elation, fulfilment and unfettered spiritual intimacy that we will love and cherish as a foretaste of Heaven itself. Then other days will arrive of toil and tedium, bruises and burdens that will seem too heavy for our ladened backs and we will struggle to keep pushing on towards the long-anticipated end. Maybe that's why you're holding this book – because you are struggling now. Who would have thought that when you started with all that enthusiasm all those years ago? But here you are, hanging on and wondering how to take that next purposeful stride.

Often we feel that this earthly leg of the journey is incessant in nature and Heaven feels as far away as it can possibly be. Our days are long, and progress is painstakingly slow and in the meantime we have lost the imminence of the New World. Our technicolour future plays no part in our grey present. We know it's coming. It's just not coming anytime soon.

But what we miss in those moments of painstakingly slow progress is that life is passing fast, and much faster than maybe we have ever supposed to this point. In fact to God, as the Psalms reveal, 1000 years is less than a watch in the night (Ps. 90:4), which means that your life to Him is merely a blink. In real terms your Christian journey is a little like setting off on a long, winding and seemingly never-ending road trip and yet, much sooner than we thought, we are there. We have made it. We rise over the hill, round the last corner and there it is before us...home! The place we have longed for, the destination we craved, and the life for which we were made.

Journeying to Heaven is the theme of this book. Indeed, journeying to Heaven needs to be the theme of your life. It is why you are here, and why you still have breath in your lungs. You were born into this world that you might spend your days travelling out of this world and to do anything else is to waste your one shot at getting it right. This is a voyage that leads you beyond time and all the pain that you can barely endure, and right into the home of God.

Let that sink in for a second so that the hope which is found in that truth can brighten the dreary vista that is currently before you. May it propel you onwards even today in the middle of whatever is unfolding, or call you to begin no matter what you are facing. We are talking about a journey that leads to paradise (Luke 23:43) where sorrows cease and tears dry (Rev. 21:4), a journey to an eternal dwelling that an eternal architect has put together for you. Moreover, it is nearer than we think and the journey to get there can be shared with Him. Every step, twist, and bump on the road can be a moment when God is right there with you. The God of the heavens can be our God in the mud. We can know Him, walk with Him through the mess and experience the joy which He alone provides. Wasn't that the experience of those who lived through the days of revival on the Island of Lewis, Scotland? They met with God in the ordinary. He was present at their kitchen tables. He was there as they worked in their fields. He was suddenly interrupting the monotonous and going with them into all the bits and pieces of life...and they loved it. God was really there. It therefore goes without saying that I hope this is your journey; that the pages of this book are a retelling of your story and your own ascent as you head to the greatest destination of all.

Or perhaps it isn't yet, but it will be. Maybe you are about to begin!

Aimlessness

Every day finds us running in dozens of directions. Life is cluttered and frenetic, burgeoning with to-do's. It is untidy. It never fits neatly into a ribboned box. Often it is sad and sore but we smother those feelings by busying ourselves even more and occupying our minds. Distracted is sadly our new normal. There is always a smart phone to hold which, according to Apple, we unlock approximately eighty times every single day.[3] The same research even suggested that when we don't unlock our phones we are still looking at them, touching them approximately 2600 times daily. Within three seconds of an app alerting us we are immersed, numbed and pulled away from our journeying status.

Alongside inane distractions are the serious ones. Projects at work that carry great importance, or family life in all of its seasons and shades. There are times when we feel we are being drawn down an endless stress-filled street, with a foreboding sense that we aren't getting anywhere. On one level we can be feverishly active and yet on another, we wonder if there is any direction to any of this. Where am I going? Who knows? What is my life for and why am I here?

Perhaps as Christians we used to know but that clarity has been stolen and now we feel like at any given moment we will step on the snake and slide back down the board

3 Knapp, J. and Zeratsky, J. *Make Time: How to Focus on What Matters Every Day* (Bantam Press, 2018), 16..

– right back to the start. Or like being on a treadmill and running hard but getting off covered in perspiration at the exact same spot you climbed on. Life can feel like that sometimes, even for followers of Jesus Christ!

I think I have just come through that kind of phase in my own life, which is probably one of the reasons I have found myself writing this book. I am thankful to God that it was only for a season but, although it was short-lived it was real: a time when any true sense of direction and purposeful journeying was strangely obscured to me. Please don't see a sloth in this confession for I have been busy during this season. But I guess that's the problem... busy but feeling aimless. Busy in ministry in our wonderful church and busy in family. I have functioned and faithfully fulfilled my duties in and out of our home. It's just that in the middle of it all a kind of haze came down and gradually I lost that definite purposeful walk that I once knew. When you have seen your destination and your whole life is propelling with passion towards it, and then suddenly that is no longer the case, you know something has altered! It is a felt experience. A loss. Like we are spiritually muddled and holding the map upside down. I'm sure as I write these words they will resonate with some readers. Is this where I am; somewhat lost and drifting?

If so, I am glad you are here. Glad you are holding this little volume in your hand. Many have been here before you and, I can promise you that includes some of the Christian giants you have revered. It is possible to journey with purpose for the first time and it is definitely possible to start journeying with purpose *again*. To know what your life is for and to know what today is for. To know what your story is, where it's all going, and how it all ends.

I can't promise you a flower-lined straight road, but I can promise you one where there is a Companion, Guide, and constant Faithful Traveller who will pull you on and light the way as the greatest Shepherd of all. And I can also promise that the destination will be worth it.

The Way

I first thought of writing this book when my eye caught sight of a nickname in the Bible. It immediately struck me as a perfect description of the life that I craved.

To be honest, I have had multiple nicknames and most of them are not repeatable here. Not by a long shot. I'm sure you have had a good few as well over the course of your life. Thankfully, virtually all of them were during my school years and have faded from memory with the passing of time.

In Bible times there were some original nicknames doing the rounds among the people of God. James and John, for instance, were dubbed 'the Sons of Thunder' in Mark 3:17, presumably because they were rather explosive in nature. Their fuse was short and on occasions the sparks would fly.

Moreover, in the early church days of Acts when new converts were facing the ire of society, there was a man named Joseph who always seemed to have the right word at the right time. He encouraged people. He put his arm around the shoulders of the weak and told them to 'keep going' when their every impulse was screaming out to chuck it in. He too got his nickname as he became known as 'Barnabas' which means 'son of encouragement.'

As I've said, this book revolves around a nickname of sorts. It's never been my nickname but I wish it had. If someone hung it over me as a banner, I am at a stage in my journey when I would accept it as a badge of honour. It has nothing to do with my physical appearance or what my surname denotes and for once it's not derogatory at all. Nevertheless, I want it to describe me for the rest of my life and fit who it is that I have become in Jesus. It's found in the book of Acts where we read that the early Christians were nicknamed as:

> ... *followers of* The Way. (Acts 9:1, 2; 19:9; 23; 22:4; 24:14, 22).

A beautiful phrase that captures the true essence of Christian discipleship both then and now. A label that takes the hugeness of the Christian life and compresses it down to a bite-sized form that makes such sense to us all. Notice what they were known for:

- Where they were going, and not where they'd been.
- Who they were following, and not who they were.
- How they were living, and not how they looked.

How wonderful!

- Known for being on the way to Heaven, not known anymore for their sinful pasts.
- Known for following their wonderful leader Jesus who IS 'the way', not known anymore by their qualities or lack thereof.
- Known by their Godly lifestyles, not known anymore by passing trends.

They may have been called this by others but so taken were they with the expression that on occasion they gladly used it themselves. Take Paul's defence, for instance, in Acts 24 as he bears witness to Jesus before the Roman authorities. There are no references to our modern tribal terms that define our preferred theological side. We don't find him clinging to his credentials or cowering in the corner due to the absence of them. Rather, he is shameless and his labels are much more plain and straight forward:

> I admit that I worship the God of our ancestors as *a follower of* The Way. (Acts 24:14)

In other words, I am a traveller and I admit it freely without a moment's hesitation! I am a sojourner. I am not ashamed to say that this world is not my home for I am going somewhere else, having left somewhere behind, and the route to get there is really precise. Paul was not born on this '*way*'. He was called to this '*way*'. You are not born on this '*way*' either. No one is. There is a start point, a new destination for our lives, and '*a way*' that joins the two.

The phrase, The Way, as we find it in Acts is unambiguous and it is tremendously non-PC in our modern woke culture. It is very defined. It points to an exact route. In short, the way to Heaven is The Way and there is no other way. Every sinner who starts on the road to Heaven starts, continues and ends in the same way. It's a road that we all need to travel down irrespective of nationality or background. It begins at a very narrow gate of decision and ultimately it leads us all to the door of Glory.

I'm not saying that we will all do the same things and wear the same clothes. A man said this to me recently. He actually thought that Christians had their own unique fashion and style and that we even drove the same kinds of cars! I'm not sure who he had been hanging out with but I was glad to put him right on this point. The Christians in Acts were not picked out of society and labelled because they all had a certain brand of sandal. And nor are we defined by these things. Rather, this nickname reveals that these Christians understood what being a true disciple of the Lord Jesus Christ meant: no directionless living and certainly no free spirits. There was *a way* and they were on it. They knew where they were going and they knew how to get there. Moreover, they longed to get there. Their whole life was about seeing it through and persevering on that precise trajectory right to the very end (Matt. 24:13). They had recognised that life can be full of nice things but in the end they will all be left behind and only Heaven is permanent treasure. It lasts.

Perhaps most significant of all is this: they had heard their Friend, Leader, Lord and Saviour state that '*I am the way*' and they believed Him (John 14:6). With every ounce of their beings they had embraced Christ. In other words, it was not simply the case that Jesus got them on the way. That definitely is NOT what this nickname points to. Rather, He *was* the way. It is through Jesus we start the journey. It is with Jesus we continue the journey. And it is to Jesus we go when the earthly leg concludes.

Time to make the most of time

For you this book may call you to begin this journey with Christ for the very first time. You may not be a Christian. Not yet! You may have never heard these things before or perhaps we did and walked away. You will read these pages and say to yourself:

'I have not even started yet.'

'What have I been doing for all of these years?'

'I have lived in the mist.'

'I have travelled, but not one inch of my journeying has been with Jesus and I am not any closer to Heaven.'

'I have no sense of purpose to my life.'

To this point you have not grasped that Jesus Christ is a real person, and that He Himself is '*the way*.' That is the marrow of Christianity. It is all about Jesus and Jesus alone. Your experience of 'faith' has maybe not portrayed that to you and instinctively you know that culture has again no room in the Inn for a unique Jesus. The title of D. A. Carson's book *The Intolerance of Tolerance* is a perfect description of where we have landed.[4] Our newfound 'tolerance' of all creeds and lifestyles has no tolerance at all for an exclusive route to Heaven. We will tolerate anything – except this! And yet that is the heartbeat of this book. To be with Christ and to follow Him is to journey on the one road that quenches the human thirst and ultimately leads to the most joyful goal of all.

Or you may read on and perhaps discover that you have got lost. You started well. You really did. You burst out of your starting blocks like an Olympic sprinter. Other Christian travellers on the road seemed to be tired by comparison and you blew them away with your newfound spiritual enthusiasm and vigour. You wondered why you were so sluggish or even cynical, for now your life had that purpose which the previous years didn't. You came to Christ and nothing else really mattered as much as it used to. You were all in, and you loved those times. You were

4 Carson, D.A. *The Intolerance of Tolerance*. William B Eerdmans, 2013.

finally alive and you knew it! And yet now something imperceptible has called you away. The passing of time has trimmed back your engines. Maybe a bitterness has crept in, or an idol with a shrine that you regularly visit. You've become listless and distracted. You're not sure how it started but you know there's a gulf between where you are and where you once were. In short you have been allured by Satan's counter-offer and so although you are consumed, the problem is you are no longer consumed with Christ. Nor are you driven to get home!

If someone were to ask you where Christians are heading you would give the stock answer and tell them about 'Heaven' but you know the painful truth that most days of your life don't reflect this. Your longings all reveal that you have become seduced. Which way is it? What is the route after all? Our doctrine is not driving our direction. There is no question that you are a true Christian but that experience of running on *The Way* with freedom is missing and you want it back.

I often think of that image of Jesus in Luke 9:51: 'As the time approached for Him to be taken up to Heaven, Jesus **resolutely set out** for Jerusalem.' That is a man with a purpose. Jesus here has one place in view and nothing will cause him to swerve. Has it been a long time since you were walking like that? Rapt, engrossed and blinkered?

And then no doubt there are some of us who just need to hear the words, 'keep going.' I hope you will. Not knowing what is happening around you and why it is so painful, I still want to urge you to stay the course, love Jesus, rest in His grace, and run your life's race on *The Way*. I want to be a Barnabas to you. To encourage, spur on, and tell you that it is all worth it. As someone who knows the experience of spiritual fatigue, I would love to journey with you and do what Alistair Brownlee did in the Tokyo Olympic Triathlon. Do you remember the iconic scene? His brother Jonny was running in first place on fumes. He was spent! After a 1.5km swim and 40km on a bike, he was into the last few steps of a 10km run. And then his legs went. Millions were glued to TV screens wondering what would happen next. He was weaving all over the track with buckling knees and unable to run as he once did. And then Alistair rounded the bend, saw him and without hesitating he grabbed his brother and pulled him home, literally pushing him over the line. Jonny's endurance mattered to Alistair. And your endurance matters to me. I would love for you to walk on, tired as you are. May this book galvanise you with the hope that soon we will be in the presence of the King of all kings and all our sojourning will be over.

Let the journey begin...

To every man there openeth
A way, and ways, and a way.
And the high soul climbs the high way,
And the low soul gropes the low,
And in between on the misty flats
The rest drift to and fro.
But to every man there openeth
A high way and a low -
And every man decideth the way his soul shall go.

– John Oxenham[5]

5 Kuhn, I. *By Searching* (Authentic Media, 2005), 12..

Getting Started

Exploring how the journey begins

I still remember as a young boy watching a family sail into the harbour at Musselburgh, Scotland in a boat they had handmade back home in New Zealand. Having taken the decision to leave what was normal, they headed off on a truly unforgettable round-the-world family adventure. Thousands of nautical miles lay ahead. There would be dangerous storms, technical difficulties, and many days of arduous sailing. The tales they told on arrival were truly remarkable. Spectacular sea creatures, tropical islands, and lots of different communities all formed part of their story. They stayed for a few years before boarding the boat again and sailing home around the other side of the globe. I've always thought their story makes my family holidays look rather staid (no pun intended). Crucial to their story was how they started. The safety of the boat, the provisions for the journey, and the set of their sails were everything. Because they began well, they journeyed well. They knew where they were going but more importantly they knew what was involved. There would be a cost and they had factored it in. I was privileged to stand on the coastline and watch as their epic voyage came to a successful conclusion.

Starting off well on any journey is critically important, and this is never truer than the Christian pilgrimage. The beginning must not be understated. There is a saying that 'it's not how you start, it's how you finish', but that is unhelpful in this context. Becoming a Christian and starting to travel through life with Jesus is the most momentous direction-shifting experience that is possible for us as humans in this world. We need to get it right.

Sometimes we speak of life-changing decisions and many of them are just that. We can move countries. We can choose to remain single. We may turn vegan. We may even sail around the world in our boat. However, I want to argue that Christianity is in a league all of its own. At least it's meant to be. Following Jesus is not merely an appendage to our daily routines. 'I have hobbies and relationships and career and...well let's try Jesus as well.' I have lost count of how many people who have considered coming to Jesus on these terms. If we are thinking that way we are not yet at the start gate to The Way.

The Bible captures 'the beginning' of this great journey in the starkest of terms when it describes becoming a Christian as moving from 'death' to 'life' (Ephesians 2:1-5). That is as big a change as it gets, isn't it? Two opposite conditions. Two contrasting states. If Paul, who wrote those words, was trying his upmost to play down the revolution that lies before those who wish to travel to Heaven, then on the basis of this picture he clearly failed. It may be an analogy of feeling mildly unwell before gradually recovering our full health would have been more pleasant to his readers. Surely softer language would have eased concerns. Would the Church not be bigger if he had gone with that? Or maybe switching lanes from one highway to another? Perhaps that would have been a brighter carton in which to package the gospel.

Instead, Paul chose the picture of death to describe our natural condition! A death from which we require a resurrection. Being present when someone dies is always a sobering experience. Someone can be dreadfully ill in hospital for many months but the difference between life and death when you see it is still incalculable. There is no comparing the two. As it happens, I am writing these words on the day Queen Elizabeth II has died and a palpable cloud of grief has suddenly enveloped our whole nation. Intuitively we know that her death is unfixable. She has gone. Even when we speak of her 'passing away' we are signalling that there is distance. Between the living and the dead there is a chasm. There is no middle ground. We are either one or the other.

Consider then how hugely significant it is that Paul picks these terms to show us what it takes for this journey to begin. He is saying that becoming a Christian is like being raised from the mortuary. Spiritual deadness is our natural state. We don't see the reality of God, sin, eternity, Jesus etc. These themes are alien to us. We are numb to the things we need to be alive to, estranged from our Maker and cut off. We are living life, but as dead people void of purpose and hope as we walk on another way – 'the way of destruction' (Matt. 7:13). In other words, according to the Bible we appear to be full of life and marked with vitality but in actual fact we are already on the wrong road. Worse still, there is nothing we can do about it without the help and intervention of a life-giving God. We need to be raised, raised up to a new life, to live in a new way.

The Bible also uses the metaphor of eyesight (or lack of) to unpack the same truth (John 9:39). Again, the gulf is vast for there is a whole ocean between blindness and vision. One sees the contours of a coastline, the beauty of a newborn baby, and the stars that sparkle in the night sky. One delights over the colours in a bird's feathers and the depth of field that an artist included in a painting. But by contrast when we are blind – we see nothing. Nothing at all. There is a shroud that conceals the joys before us. Our eyes have been veiled and we miss what is patently obvious to others.

Consider how the Bible defines us in our natural state:

- We are alienated from God (Col. 1:21).
- We engage in evil behaviour (Col. 1:21).
- We are dead in our trespasses and sins (Eph. 2:1).
- We follow the ways of the world (Eph. 2:2).
- We gratify our sinful cravings (Eph. 2:3).
- We are deserving of the wrath of God (Eph. 2:3).
- We do not believe in Jesus as Saviour (John 5:38).
- We are blinded by the god of this world (2 Cor. 4:4).
- We are lawless and darkened (2 Cor. 6:14-15).
- We are already judged as guilty by God (John 3:18).

- We are oblivious to the danger we are in (Luke 12:46).
- We are destined to be judged on the last day (John 12:48).
- We have rejected Jesus (John 12:48).

Be Cautious

For some of us the possibility of transformation will be music to our ears for our lives right now are in such bad shape that the thought of radical change pricks our attention. Perhaps life so far has been deeply cruel. You may sadly be one of the many silent sufferers of abuse, either in adult years or back in a childhood that was filled with chaos and rejection. Your life experiences may have been so deeply painful that you are fearful to recount them to others. You may have tried to forget and move on and even satisfy yourself with interests, relationships and more possessions but you just haven't been able to. You are maybe like one young man who went to University and lived for lust but ended up broken, primed and ready for the newness of life that Jesus offers. His name was Augustine and it was his inner ache for fulfilment that readied him for the transformative offer of the Gospel[1].

It could be that this is you; longing for something that so far you have currently been unable to enjoy. A lingering emptiness. You may not know fully all that is entailed on The Way but the concept at least is appealing.

Others by contrast will feel hesitant. Indeed, quite possibly you may feel you don't need to be changed at all.

---

1 Brown, P *Augustine of Hippo – A Biography,* University of California Press, 2000.

A friend of mine was recently talking to another man in a launderette about Jesus and this was precisely the man's response; that all the Christians he had met had a need for change because they were financially poor, addicted, or buffeted by the wildness of life. There was a throbbing pain and Jesus would prove to be a great crutch. Another junkie 'finding God.' But by contrast he was fine, or so he thought. He didn't feel he had a need. His car was sitting outside and his career was on the up. Life was good and Jesus wasn't required. He had all his ducks in a row and he felt pretty smug about it too. He had concluded that change would be folly when things were apparently going so well.

Well, wherever you are in life at this point you need to understand that life with Jesus is more than bettering yourself and escaping life's cruel blows. Be cautious of that approach. It is also more than the injection of happiness. You need to grasp at the start of this journey that the work of redemption is deeper. You are not just an injured person. Nor are you merely broken, as painful as that is. These terms are helpful but they do not fully define you. Rather, you are dead and blind. You desperately need to be raised and you need sight. Jesus is required, not to better you but to save you.

I want to emphasise this for unless we have come to see that this *way* begins with a resurrection, then we have probably not understood the gospel of Jesus Christ at all. I grew up in an era when evangelism (well-meaning though it was) revolved around issuing 'a call' for sinners to pray a prayer or raise a hand in a meeting as the preacher brought the sermon to a climax. I have no doubt that many were truly converted at these events. Indeed, my own conversion stems back to a similar occasion. I walked to the front of a meeting with my mother by my side as I gave my life to Jesus.

However, with many genuine conversions came many spurious ones. There was no question these people responded. There is also no question that they meant it. Perhaps their emotions had been piqued or maybe they wanted the change in life we have described above and here it was being offered to them. But what was missing was an honest explanation of what they were leaving and why. The start was obscured. Therefore, as Jesus puts it, 'When trouble or persecution come because of the word they quickly fall away' (Mark 4:17).

Worse still are the countless numbers of people who hold on to a decision they made way back in their teens at an evangelistic meeting. Yet nothing since then has changed at all. They went on to live with a false assurance of Heaven when their journey since then would indicate that the beginning was bungled.

Michael Lawrence helpfully speaks of the need for 'real repentance'[2] and warns that anything less than 'turning to love God, whom we formerly hated' will be nothing more than a brief spiritual encounter. What does a false convert look like? Often, he says, it is someone who:

- is excited about Heaven, but bored by Christians and the local church.

- thinks Heaven will be great purely because their relatives / friends will be there. Seeing Jesus is not on their radar.

---

2 Lawrence, M. *How God Creates a People* (Crossway, 2017), 31.

- likes Jesus, but didn't sign up for the rest – obedience, holiness, discipleship, suffering.
- can't tell the difference between obedience motivated by love and legalism.
- is bothered by other people's sins more than his or her own.
- holds grace cheap and his own comfort costly.

On the other hand, the genuine Christian is someone who

- loves fellow Christians and the local church because he or she loves God (1 John 5:1).
- longs for fellowship with God and not just ease in Heaven (1 John 1:6-7).
- understands that following Jesus means discipleship (1 John 1:6).
- obeys God out of love for God (1 John 5:2-3).
- is eager to confess and turn away from his or her sin (1 John 1:9).
- views grace as costly and his own desires as cheap (1 John 1:7,10).

Starting Well

As I write this I am not at home. We have travelled as a family for a break on the Scottish west coast and we did not travel light. With many humans plus two dogs – Molly and Mabel – in tow, and the need to factor in the unpredictable nature of Scotland's climate, we have come prepared for all possibilities. In short, we have luggage and lots of it. If we decide to stay for the next 12 months or live through several more lockdowns I think we would pull through.

While most journeys begin with the question, 'what will I take?', the Christian journey is utterly unique. The question is, 'what must I leave?' What is superfluous? Being honest (and this will be hard to take for those who are not yet Christians), all the cases and bags that you carried as part of your 'deadness' must now be abandoned. The Apostle Paul depicts this perfectly for us as he describes his luggage-free hands when he came to the start of The Way:

> For whatever was to my profit I now consider loss for the sake of Christ. What is more I consider everything a loss compared to the surpassing greatness of knowing Christ Jesus my Lord, for whose sake I have lost all things. I consider them rubbish that I may gain Christ. (Phil. 3:7-8)

Here is a man who is leaving everything. He knows that one world is being left and another is being embraced. Deadness and blindness are giving way to life and vision. Moreover, notice what is swapped in this great exchange: he is losing all of his 'profit' (what he used to live for) for one person – Christ! Is he being serious? Is Jesus really that valuable? Are you willing to trade what you once clung onto for meaning, hope, and fulfilment so that Christ and Christ alone is your true treasure?

If we are in any doubt about the change before us then prior to going any further we need to get it clear. Jesus is the prize being offered and whatever it means for you, the Bible claims He is worth it. Paul has weighed it all up and considered that gaining Jesus is better than holding onto that which has failed him thus far. Indeed, should he 'gain the whole world and forfeit his soul' (Matt. 16:26) he will end with nothing.

We will come to this in future chapters but it is vital we grasp that this is the heart of all of the change that comes to those who embark on this new way. They have reached a gate and to pass through it they are willing to jettison all their old idols for one new love. Jesus is that new love. They have judged Him to be worth losing all.

With this concept of 'left luggage' in mind we need to examine a few of the life-changing steps that everyone will take as they embark on The Way to Heaven itself.

Richard Sibbs understood the importance of this when he said: 'He that never knew the 'height, and breadth, and depth of his natural corruption, will never be able to conceive of the height, and breadth, and depth of God's infinite love in Jesus Christ.'[3] In other words, to Sibbs the way we view Jesus and the way we value grace all stems from the way we view ourselves. If all that's required is a helping hand, or a little dusting off to get us started on The Way, then we will end up with a very small and unworthy Christ. Grace will be cheapened. Salvation will be diminished, and moreover our joy will be quenched.

We must stare in the mirror and see ourselves. Only then will we behold the true wonder of what God is offering. Whether we are a child of the manse as I was or someone who has lived as far away from church as is humanly possible, we must all enter in by this 'narrow

3 Sibbs, R. *The Complete Works of Richard Sibbs* (Edinburgh: Banner of Truth, 2023), 14.

gate' (Matt. 7:13, 14). The start is the same for us all. The following chapters unpack what is involved when we move from 'death' to 'life' and from 'blindness' to 'vision' and I urge you to pause and make sure that you have begun as you should.

Chapter One

A Great Dilemma

'The fool says in his heart, "There is no God"'

Psalm 14:1

God!

This is where it all begins. Before anything else and before asking all the other niggling questions that we will want to have answered, we must settle this issue that weaves its way into every part of our lives in this world – is there a God and if so, can I know Him? One who sees me today, understands me intimately, and loves me more than it is possible for me to fully understand. And is it really the truth that this God is beckoning me to Himself; to come to Him as I am, follow Him on The Way, and entrust my entire existence into His hands?

For millions of people, and perhaps even yourself, God is currently not in the picture and not even on the outer edges! In an article in the Guardian newspaper, UK, on the growing trends of unbelief, Adam Cardone from New York City spoke for many when he said, 'I only know one

God, and that's me. I am responsible for my own destiny.'[1] Such people live without God, don't believe in Him, and nor do they seem to care. When a recent visitor to our home spoke about the sudden death of his two parents he looked up to the sky, put out his two hands, and said, 'Where was God in that?' He is an ardent unbeliever.

Even a reverence towards God which used to mark Western culture has been replaced with an avalanche of ambivalence and incredulity. Phrases like 'the man upstairs' are increasingly common. I recently spoke to my neighbour about God and he responded politely with the curt statement, 'I don't do that.' In other words, he doesn't 'do' God. To him, God is like the dodo. He is extinct. Dead! Or perhaps that is doing the dodo a disservice for there actually was something called the dodo on this planet. By contrast, God, for many, is just a figment of one's imagination. Maybe the unicorn is a better analogy; God is a nice thought with no substance.

The daily news these days may be full of war in Europe, a cost of living crisis, political uncertainty and the lingering fumes of a global pandemic, but God is not even in the conversation. There are no news anchors cutting to an outside broadcast where the words of God are given to the watching anxious viewers. The same could be said of our schools. God is gagged, silenced and seen as an irritating intruder into our daily existence. A recent YouGov Poll[2] in the UK evidenced this, finding that 4 in 10 Britons believe there is neither 'a God' nor 'a higher power'. Incredibly, among those who identify as Christians, just over half (51%) believe in the existence

1 Cardone, A. 'I only know one God'. The Guardian Newspaper, 23 Jan 21.

2 YouGov Poll, 27-30 Nov 2020 'Christianity Study'.

of God. To put that statistic the correct way round, some 49% of British people who label themselves as Christians are also identifying as atheists. I don't think I'm articulate enough to explain how that is even possible other than to say that these people are sadly still spiritually dead and blind. In a world where something is only true if it can be proven scientifically, there simply isn't a category for the God of the Bible anymore and to state otherwise is guaranteed to lead to someone saying, "Prove it."

In many respects we can relate to this caution for when we hear of something which seems like a stretch we do like to benefit from solid irrefutable data. We understand that evidence is what takes us from sceptics to believers. We want the concrete reassurance that facts bring to us. If I told you, for instance, that next week I am flying to the moon you would be very gullible and possess extraordinary faith if you didn't want to see my spacesuit and ticket. We like the tangible. We need it. There are lots of tall stories around, and with the physical and concrete to rely on we believe we won't be duped.

Isobel Kuhn, who gave up a comfortable life to serve God in South-West China, was once one of these sceptics. In her freshman class her atheistic teacher, Dr Sedgewick, opened his lecture by asking the students, 'Is there anyone here who believes there is a Heaven or Hell and the story of Genesis is true? Please raise your hand.' Isobel, along with only one other student, put her hand up. Dr Sedgewick smiled and said to the two students, 'Oh, you only believe that because your papa and mama told you so.'[3] It was an experience that led Isobel into doubt

3 Kuhn, I. *By Searching* (Authentic Media, 2005), 7.

before true assurance finally came to her. She had to know for herself.

No Sense to Non-Belief

Please consider for a moment what Andrew Wilson notes in response to our questions:

> Take the statement: "For something to be true, it must be provable scientifically." Can that statement be proved scientifically? Can you do an experiment in a lab to prove that is true? Or how about, "my daughter loves me"? How can that very important statement ever be proven? The fact is, we believe things because they make sense of the world as we see it, not because some outside authority (like scientific proof) says they are true. So the real question is: How does belief or non-belief in God make sense of the world around us?[4]

Surely this is a critical perspective that our world needs to engage with, and so do you. When you open the Bible you will discover that it doesn't feel a need to prove anything at all. God isn't on trial. Rather, it begins with the news that there is a Maker. Genesis impresses upon us in the plainest of terms that God is! He exists! In fact, as Andrew Wilson argues, to say otherwise makes no sense of tides, planets, mohawk eagles and 7.77 million other species for where have they come from? There is a precision and a designer's hand all over our world, an artist's touch. As I write this much of North America and Mexico has marvelled as our moon has glided with exactness over the sun, causing the earth beneath to be plunged into darkness. Do we really believe that these two heavenly bodies were flung into

4 Wilson, A. *Incomparable* (David C. Cook, 2008), 8.

space by a cosmic mega-charged explosion and now they can coalesce like this? Can our 'faith' stretch this far? To argue in this vein, whether passively or intentionally, is in some small sense the same as admiring your IKEA furnishings and concluding that a big bang in Sweden caused them. There was an explosion in a forest and, hey presto, out came your perfectly engineered Poàng armchair! Can we really look at our world and all that is in it and confidently remain as 'nonbelievers'?

Not so long ago a ticket to fly on Jeff Bezos's space rocket was purchased by a thrill seeker for $28 million. Now let's just say we hitched a ride ourselves and hurtled towards space with Mr Bezos at a speed of just over 38,500 miles per hour, setting our coordinates for Proximus Centauri. Keep in mind, this is the closest star that we know of to our own galaxy's sun and that there are billions which are millions of light years further away. That journey (which is some 4.2 million light years from where you are currently sitting) would take us 88,000 years. Please pause and let that hit you. The vastness of our Universe is staggering. It is beyond our comprehension. Our Universe is a complex, spectacular, and ordered work of art.

Can you bring yourself to say that all this just happened and fell into place? Could something as dependable and exact as the gravitational pull of our moon which holds the oceans in check, miraculously come from the chaos of a cosmic bang?

Or take the four chambers of your own heart and how they function with such efficiency and regularity that your heart beats 100,000 times each day, pumping 5 litres of blood at any given moment. This is extraordinary. If a human came up with this they would be knighted and lauded. We would clamour around such a creator.

However, our deadness and blindness is such that we believe this has just happened. We are here by chance, the product of fortuitous events. Being honest, does it not take more faith to believe in nothing than it does to be believe in Someone – Someone who has caused this, and brought all this into existence.

Lee Strobel, the atheistic journalist, who sought to prove that God didn't exist only to become a Christian himself, was deeply moved when he read Sir John Templeton's famous quotation: 'Would it not be strange if a universe without purpose, accidentally created humans who are so obsessed with purpose?'[5] Strange indeed! The existence of purpose-seeking humans who have a purposeless origin surely makes no sense at all.

In the beginning God

Your journey to Heaven, therefore, needs to begin right here with God. It must! It is the starting point in the Bible, the starting point for the Universe, and now it must be the starting point for this voyage before you. Having said that, the Bible is clear that belief in God is not enough, in and of itself, to take you to Heaven, for even the demons believe (James 2:19) and they are certainly not on The Way. You can believe in God and still not be a Christian. However, you can't be a Christian and not believe in God.

God, as the Bible presents Him, is simply amazing! So glorious and other worldly that to write about Him is almost to misrepresent Him. We should tread with caution at this point and flee from the danger of restricting Him by our own experience or our limited grasp of English. To illustrate this, I may think Kenya is the most beautiful

---

5 Strobel, L. *The Case for Christ* (Zondervan, 1998), 7.

place I have been to and yet I would fail miserably to unpack its wonder with words. Postcards fall painfully short and so do our holiday stories. It is better that you go to see for yourself.

Do you understand that God is like that? The Bible bids us to move beyond descriptions and language and to 'taste and see (for ourselves) that the Lord is good' (Ps. 34:8); to experience Him, and plunge ourselves into His inexhaustible perfections and find that there is no part of Him that disappoints.

One of the magnificent themes of the Bible is that God wants to be known. He wants us to behold Him. He longs for us to be with Him, marvel and spend our lives pursuing a deeper understanding of who He is and what He does. We were made to enjoy Him and satisfy our lives in Him forever. I have known people who have suffered from Anthropophobia (the crippling fear of people) and they literally never leave their home in case they end up being too close to others. Humans must be avoided at all costs. However, we can be absolutely sure that God does not suffer from those symptoms. Indeed what the Bible records for us is a God who draws near despite the mess that He finds in our lives. He seems magnetised to the weary and broken-hearted. He is there in the Garden of Eden, and again in the giving of the 10 Commandments, and again as the Israelites wander, and again in the story of prophets, and then ultimately when Jesus steps right into history, He is there. At that point we hear the words from Jesus' lips that 'Anyone who has seen me has seen the Father'. (John 14:9)

The tabernacle in the Old Testament was the place, within the camp of the Israelites, in which God was said to presence Himself. It was the sign that He was there and among them. The Israelite community would look to this tent and know deep within themselves that they were not alone for God had drawn near. Remarkably, this word for 'tabernacle' crops up in the New Testament when John is recording his Gospel. Speaking of Jesus he says that 'the Word became flesh and made *his dwelling* (tabernacle) among us.' Again He was drawing near. God was close. As we shall see as we move on in this journey, one of the greatest wonders that awaits new Christians is that God makes us His tabernacle. He indwells us. His Spirit is given as He makes us His home.

Here then is a God who speaks, reveals Himself and is near to humans. God is accessible. He is approachable. We could go as far as to say that He is sociable and enjoys being in the midst of His creation. His other-worldliness means we could never reach up to Him but what we find is He has reached down to us. We will never plumb the depths of all that He is but we are invited to spend our lives digging and searching for more of His beauty.

For many of us our concept of God will be far removed from what the Bible reveals. Perhaps we will need to start all over again and put to death the false god we have imagined. Most of us like to have a god on standby. A little god we can pull out of our pockets in the case of emergencies. Like a genie from a lamp we like to keep Him in there when He is unwanted and call Him out when He is.

Many others, by contrast, may have pictured a capricious tyrant who is ambivalent to our suffering and so inept he is unable to do anything about it. Perhaps we suffered at the hands of a cruel earthly father and that experience has shaped our ideas of what this Heavenly Father might be like. We are wary of Him and wonder if

He is detached from us. Is He uncaring and unmoved by humanity's plight? He may be 'there'. However, 'there' is so far away that it feels He is not here.

Or maybe we feel that, if there is a God who has made planets, stars and life then He is surely too great to stoop and relate to someone like you. Sadly, even churches have presented this kind of distant fearful being, and in the end the 'knowability' of God has been lost along the way. Therefore, please grasp the wonderful news that the Bible presents. The journey to Heaven is actually a journey with company. It is a journey into God as we delve deeper into Him, and it is a journey with God as we share every step of The Way.

Again, to stress, you can believe in Him and still not be a Christian. There are many millions of people in our world who have a belief in some kind of higher power, and they have convinced themselves that they are on The Way. Sadly, as their lives reveal, they are not, and what is missing is the gospel. Nevertheless, to be a Christian you must begin here. God is real! We are not alone. He is breathtaking, unchanging in His nature, eternal in His span, sovereign over all, and loving to His creation. He wants to make Himself known to you.

Chapter Two

A Great Creator

'You knit me together in my mother's womb'

Psalm 139:13

Thirty-two years ago I made a TV cabinet in my school woodwork class and I loved it. The hinges were a little shoddy and I remember one of the doors was planed a shade too vociferously which meant that it never quite closed properly. I had spent months putting it together with chisels, hammers, a vice, screws, and eventually some varnish to finish it off. From memory my long-suffering teacher gave me a C+ for my workmanship which reveals what an impressive piece it was. He clearly didn't have an eye for talent! And yet I still remember to this day carrying it home and proudly setting it down in the corner of our family living room in Edinburgh. Our little square Hitachi TV sat on top and the VCR recorder even had its own shelf! It was flawed but it was loved. When visitors came round to our home I would be glad when the conversation eventually got round to the one-of-a-kind unit in the corner and with a sense of pride I would tell them it was mine.

In a world where dignity and worth have often been stripped from human beings, it is tremendously important that we pause here and allow ourselves to be overwhelmed with the white-hot love that God has for what *He* has made. Loving a flawed cabinet is one thing. Loving a person that you have planned, designed, and fashioned is another. Right down to your height, facial features, eye colour and gender, you are the product of the weaving hand of God who has made you precisely as He intended. All that you saw this morning as you looked in the mirror, whether it pleased you or not, is the handiwork of an architect who is not prone to producing flawed exhibits. When God creates there are no C+ grades to be found. In fact, at the conclusion of the creation narrative in Genesis when God saw the wonders that had come from His hands, He made the sweeping declaration that it was 'very good' (Gen. 1:31). He was so pleased. He needed no erasers and there were no discarded piles of dross lying at the side of Eden that day. It may be that our world (and you) has changed the goalposts in defining what beauty is and who it is that has more worth than others, but God is unmoved. He loves His stunning world. And He loves you. The magazines may airbrush and the advertisements may push a stereotype of what is attractive, but God has knit you together and still finds pleasure in you, even the flawed version of you that is marred with sin. He looks over our lives and His joyous heart declares 'you are mine!'

John Piper captured this in a sermon he preached in 1987 entitled 'The Pleasure of God in His Creation.'[1] I wonder how differently that statement would read were

1 Piper, J The Pleasure of God in His Creation. Sermon 1987. https://www.desiringgod.org/messages/the-pleasure-of-god-in-his-creation.

it to relate to ourselves: 'the pleasure of Graham in'...How would it end? Or what would our family record as being the source of pleasure that we experience in this world? Perhaps, 'the pleasure of Graham in sports.' Or maybe, 'the pleasure of Graham in his own reputation.' Perhaps for some of us, it is the pleasure we find in amassing our money. We are so drawn to what is temporal and passing. We are living in paradise, surrounded by 7 billion living and breathing masterpieces and everyday we seem to miss it. The world and its contents have lost their sparkle. The stars twinkle, the waves roll in, and babies gurgle, but we have seen it before. What a wonderful experience it would be if God allowed us to stare at the world as though it was created yesterday. As if today was our first time opening our curtains and seeing a tree, or a playful robin. Or maybe this evening we would meet a person for the first time and the encounter flooded our hearts with pleasure as we admired the wisdom and power of God.

The great news is that God has not grown tired of what He has made. It is because He has made you that He finds pleasure in you. You have come from Him. He views your little life today as treasure and He is drawn to you. I'm not sure what it is that has caused us to lose this understanding of the character of God but there is no question that we have, and instead we have replaced it with something that is deeply dangerous. Most of us now have an inbuilt urge to view the love of God as something that is earned and a commodity that ebbs and flows depending on the way we live or who we are, as if the love of God is contingent, and my life is the determining factor. If I do well today He will treasure me. If I don't, He will look away in disgust. Perhaps the flakiness of the world's love around us has infiltrated our thinking and now we believe that only the picture-perfect life is delighted over in Heaven. Not so!

Just prior to writing this chapter Mabel, one of our dogs, ran away from home in order to pursue a better life. We were at a wedding reception when we learned that she had checked out and by the time we returned home she was off on her epic adventure, even choosing to swim in the sea at one stage. We came back to find that our local community had sprung into action in order to aid the rescue attempt. Strangers had left the comfort of their homes in response to a post we had put on social media and were frantically searching for her. There were dozens of people we had never met. A man even came from the other side of the city with a thermal imaging drone in order to join the hunt. When we eventually got her home and reflected on the kindness and concern that neighbours, friends and dog lovers had shown to us we were genuinely humbled. There was an outpouring of emotions and relief when she was located and all was well.

Dogs are amazing, but they are not in the same league as humans. They are not in your league. If we love our dogs, how much more should we love the apex of all that God has made. And how much more does God love us. Indeed, is it not a sign of where we are in society that a missing dog will get us out of our chairs and raise our heartbeat, and yet babies being aborted will not? Have we not lost a sense of wonder and awe over mankind? I want you to walk away from reading this chapter and know that however you look and whatever the number of likes your latest post generated on social media, your God is finding pleasure in your existence.

A Redemption Plan

What we now need to see is that all this explains the gospel story and the rescuing, redeeming heart of God for His world...and for you! God is not an intruder or a nuisance. He is an owner, and as an owner He wants something back. He longs for it. What was once His has been lost and He is employing all of His love to reclaim it and draw us again into His warm embrace.

Moreover, His intention is something more wonderful than a reunion. It is restoration. Your restoration. Humanity has been sullied and defiled by Adam's rejection of God in Eden. Our forerunner fell and with him we all fell, and God has seen fit to judge the whole created order. The original beauty can still be seen in sunsets, the array of colours in a fruit stall, and even in dog-loving rescuers, but our world and everything in it is creaking. It is not what it once was. My career in social work prior to ministry revealed a lurking evil in the heart of humans, much of which would be irresponsible to divulge on these pages but, suffice to say, man's inhumanity to his fellow man is astounding. We are so terribly flawed, and every part of us is affected. And yet God is intent on renewal. He is resolved to one day bring an end to the groaning of creation itself, and even to bring an end to your suffering, sin and tears. He is driven by love for all He has made.

I'm sure as you are reading this your body and soul are far from the two perfect specimens who walk across the pages of creation's story in Genesis. There we find Adam and Eve in straight-from-the-wrapper condition. They are free from the bodily fragility that mark us today; unsullied by disease and unimpeded by decay. This is not our story.

Not long ago I took a call from my best friend whose mother has been dreadfully ill over the last number of weeks. He described to me how he was permitted to speak to her in the theatre prior to major surgery as the surgeon was concerned she would not pull through. It seemed that the end was coming and that time was short. He prayed with her and then had to let go of her hand as the medical staff took over. All he could do was retreat to the car park outside and beg God for her life. Does this scene resemble a masterpiece? It doesn't! Our existence is now much closer to the battered cabinet that sat in the corner of our living room all those years ago. We are somewhat bevelled, weak, twisted and full of imperfections. Some are obvious to the naked eye but others are much more deeply rooted and hidden in the turmoil of brittle minds.

And then there are our souls which, as we have seen, are so far from our Maker that we are dead and blind. We worship the created and not the creator and have idols that do not quench the longings in our lives. We are seeking but not finding. We lack direction and a sense of purpose evades us.

Has God abandoned us? Have we drifted so far that He has washed His hands and left us to destroy ourselves in our own sinfulness? Is there no hope for us? No way back from the destruction that we have caused? I am thankful that the gospel is transformative and it is also restorative. Praise God it promises a new world and it offers a new life that is so complete that one day all our flaws, body and soul, will be wiped away.

The Maker

As we end this chapter I want you to think of Isaiah looking up to the heavens on a starry night in Isaiah 40:26,

> 'Lift up your eyes on high and see: who created these? He who brings out their host by number, calling them all by name; by the greatness of his might, and because he is strong in power not one is missing.'

Here is a man whose heart had not grown used to the world around him. He was still stunned and awe-struck by what was before him as he stopped to look up and stare. I'm not sure what he would have expressed had he the benefit of telescopes that could take him deeper into the unfathomable vastness of space. And yet, look again at what it is that has gripped him. Look at what is truly awesome. He says, "Lift up your eyes on high and see: ***who created all these***?"

That is the issue, isn't it? In other words, if creation is stunning what is the creator Himself like? How glorious and worthy of the undivided loyalty and devotion of our lives must He be? God's power has taken Isaiah's breath away and he echoes what is said, several millennia later, when some fishermen witness a Galilean still the storm before their eyes. 'Who is this', they say, 'for even the winds and the waves obey him?' (Matt. 8:27)

Who is this?

If my cabinet was flawed because I am, then God's creation is stunning because He is. It is a reflection of His character, displaying variety and beauty because He is more beautiful than we have ever conceived in our finite minds. Creation, even in its flawed state, is still shouting this out to us. 'Who is this?' 'Who created all these?' God means for us to be amazed at what He has done, but not for the sake of creation itself. It is so that we will look beyond it, and see in it that God is deserving of all that we are and more. When you come to the start of the journey to Heaven you are coming to God. To the God who loves His creation. And you are coming to be astounded by Him. As John Piper says in his sermon, 'In the end, it will not be the seas or the mountains or the canyons or the clouds or the great galaxies that fill our hearts to breaking with wonder and fill our mouths with eternal praise. It will be God himself.'[2]

---

2 Ibid.

Chapter Three

A Great Fall

'There is no one righteous, not even one'

Romans 3:10

Who do you *think* you are? That's quite a question for all of us to consider as we come to one of the central planks in this unfolding gospel story. Who you really are and who you *think* you are, are usually two very different considerations and often a vast gulf will exist between the two. For instance, I may think of myself as one of the finest golfers to ever walk on our famous Scottish fairways and I may even tell that to everyone who will listen. And yet what I think and who I really am are not the best of bedfellows in my case. There is a chasm between my prideful thoughts and reality. You will recall in our 'Getting Started' chapter that the man my friend met in the launderette also had thoughts of himself that probably represent many of us reading these pages. He was keen that day to present the best version of himself and so would have said something like: 'I am successful, happy, self-sufficient, content and I certainly wouldn't class myself as needy. That's how I think of myself. That's who I am.'

However, what this man *thinks* about himself is sadly not reflective of the Bible's message. It is certainly not what his creator thinks either. As we will see shortly, our need is deeply profound and if we think of ourselves more highly than we ought we will always struggle to fully comprehend why Jesus had to come into our world and how any of this has relevance to our lives.

It may well be helpful to note in passing here, before we begin, that many of us are already struggling with our thought lives for very different reasons. Sadly we are not short on crippling feelings of self-loathing and anxiety is never far from our door. I was visiting a church recently where I heard someone describing his lifelong struggle with self-critical thoughts. In short, he found it hard to like himself. And he is not alone in this.

Because of that we may be wondering why a chapter that views us *negatively* is required. For years we may have had to create a public persona that conceals what we really think of ourselves and it has been truly exhausting hiding our pain. Our turmoil may be private but it is real; we spend our lives masking who we know ourselves to be. On the surface we appear together, confident and content but under the hood of this façade we are falling apart. I recently read Dr Neil Anderson's account of a counselling session with a 17-year-old who seemed to have the whole world at her feet.[1] She had graduated near the top of her class, had the offer of a scholarship on the table, and was also an extremely talented musician. She had also driven her parents' sports car to the appointment. And yet hidden from view was a fearful and troubled young woman who was crushed by the weight of life and her

1 Anderson, N. *Victory Over the Darkness* (Monarch, 1990), 72.

own self-criticisms. As such she regularly cried herself to sleep at night.

With that in mind I want to say to you that as we explore the 'bad news' of the gospel we need to hold it in tandem with the 'good news' that is coming. We must remember we are loved. More than you can possibly understand you are deeply valued by your Maker. There is a God in Heaven who sees you today, knows you, hears you and understands. Moreover, there is such a thing as grace as we will soon see. However, in order to see how glorious all this is we need this chapter to enable us to think accurately as we stare into the abyss of our hearts. Indeed, failure to see ourselves as we are will only serve to diminish Jesus as well as the grace He is extending to all of us. We will not see the wonders of the gospel nor experience the joy it brings to those who believe. If our need is small, then to us the gospel will be small. If our hearts are clean then the cross will seem excessive and extreme. But if we can see the magnitude of our problem, we will see Jesus in all of His glory and we will love Him all the more for what He has done.

The way up is down

Trying to convince someone of their need for Jesus when they perceive themselves as being inherently good is a particularly difficult task. They may willingly listen to the message but have no felt sense of requiring what it is that Jesus offers. There is simply no sense that they lack something, and no concept of danger. It is like persuading a sun lover to flee the beach when they don't believe the tsunami is coming. Such a person will carry on in blissful ignorance and will not understand why they would ever need a rescuing redeemer. Jesus will appear irrelevant and unnecessary. He is a crutch that isn't required.

Because of that, if we are going to travel upwards to Heaven we first need to travel down into the depths of our souls and clearly see the morass that is there. Our true identity matters. We need to face it and feel who it is that we are in the sight of God. In Genesis 3 we are suddenly informed that the idyllic world in which Adam and Eve lived had been changed forever as their intimate relationship with God was severed. God had explicitly told them, 'You must not eat from the tree of the knowledge of good and evil, for when you eat of it you will surely die' (Gen. 3:3). It was a specific rule that came from creator to creation. He who knew best and He who owned His world was informing His creation of His will for their lives.

Sadly they ate...and they died! Moreover, we all did. They didn't need the knowledge of good for they already had that, but what they got as they gained the knowledge of evil was more and worse than they could ever have imagined. The impact of their fall was so far-reaching that every subsequent member of the human race would be in their image and suffer the consequences of Eden's disobedience.

Of course we might object at this juncture and wonder why God gave humanity the choice of obedience in the first place. If God is God, we might say, then why not just insist on obedience rather than affording Adam and Eve a free will to choose. Could He not have made us incapable of evil and capable only of what is right? Would that not have resulted in less evil, pain and tears? But of course, as all of us know, what kind of love is robotic love? Or a love that is insisted upon? Or a love that is demanded? I might well have a rule in our home that every member of my family *must* express their love for me twice a day but wouldn't it be much more satisfying if they freely chose to? If their hearts leapt with affection for me and coercion wasn't required? And wouldn't our love for our Maker be deeper and marked with authenticity if we freely poured out our hearts without any strong-arm tactics?

This is the story in Genesis. Humanity has been made but now it can choose. A crossroads is before them. And as our representatives stand at the moment of decision they choose to abandon their Maker...and they die!

Two Kinds of Death

There are, in essence, two kinds of 'deaths' that are in view at this point and both will reveal humanity's plight. Of course in a physical sense it would take years for Adam and Eve to actually breathe their last, but eventually they did, and their families would lose them as they left this world, never to return. Death was not part of Eden 1.0 but suddenly it was here in our world. They were made from the dust and to dust they returned and for everyone who would come after them this same reality of limited time would cast its long shadow.

I first became aware of death when I was around six years old, often crying myself to sleep filled with fear that one day it would separate me from my two parents whom I adored. I couldn't take in the finality of it; how someone could be there and then suddenly not be. What would it feel like to be left? What would it feel like for them? For my wife, Sarah, she did not need to imagine as her own mum would suddenly be taken from her in a car accident. When Sarah went to school that morning, aged 7, she did not know that a lifetime of loss was about to open up to her and her family. Many of us reading these pages will know only too well the ache that bereavement has brought into our souls.

C. S. Lewis's journey through loss is well known due to his book, *A Grief Observed.*[2] His dear wife Joy died from cancer in July 1960 and he captured his subsequent battles with grief and loneliness, writing that 'the death of a beloved is an amputation. How often will the vast emptiness astonish me like a complete novelty and make me say, "I never realized my loss till this moment"? The same leg is cut off time after time.' In other words, for Lewis the nightmare was revisited and the pain was such that for months and years it felt like his wife had only passed yesterday. Death remained raw and it was a wound that never quite healed in this life.

Do you not long to live? To stay alive and to keep your loved ones too? Isn't it innate for us to avoid all dangers that might threaten their existence and ours? Isn't death, whether ours or those that we love, not the event that we fear the most? And does it not loom over the horizon as we age? The lengths to which we have gone during a recent global pandemic in order to preserve our lives surely reveal this to us. We willingly changed every pattern and familiar routine in order to stave off the menacing hazards. We wanted to continue on as we were in health. We sacrificed in order to live. And yet the truth is that one day we will die. It is not morbid to state it. It is simply the truth. Whether it is sudden or after a long period of slow decline we will eventually not be here in this world.

To add to this, there is a second devastating death from which we require being rescued. If the first death is physical, then this second death is spiritual for Adam and

2 Lewis, C.S. *A Grief Observed* (Faber & Faber, 2013), 56.

Eve's soul-satisfying life-giving union with God was also severed. They had once walked with Him and enjoyed the smile of His pleasure but now there was distance and judgment. Their relationship with the one who knew them the best and loved them the most was no more. They had chosen another way and while they would live for a time (physically) they would also instantly die (spiritually). As Paul puts it, 'the person without the Spirit does not accept the things that come from the Spirit of God but considers them foolishness, and cannot understand them because they are discerned only through the Spirit (1 Cor. 2:14)'. Here is the essence of this death. What once was their delight is now utter foolishness and God would be left behind. He would be shunned.

To be clear, I am not saying that unbelievers are incapable of good. In fact, we personally will know a multitude of decent, pleasant and very kind human beings who are not in church on Sundays and are not worshippers of Jesus. They are at the forefront of community initiatives and relief efforts and our world is the better for them. The reason for this is because we all are still bearing the image of our Maker and, therefore, our lives often still reflect the traits that we find in Him. But our problem is not doing good things. Our problem is enjoying God, and enjoying obeying Him. It is no longer our joy to submit to Him, to reflect Him, and to yield to Him. He is not our delight and His ways are not what we crave. In other words, we may be successful externally at keeping rules that God has instituted. We may even be kind and generous to the extreme, and dedicate our lives to doing good things. But internally our hearts are constantly pulled the other way. We remain far from Him. We don't love Him. And we don't enjoy Him. We have idols that we prefer...for we have died.

Who are you?

Here then is our problem. We are doused in splendour for the image of God marks us all and we are capable of the extraordinary. We can make, invent, ascend great heights, and create works of art that generations will marvel over. We can care. We can shower the unloved with love. We can save lives on the operating table. We can fly to space. And yet all that said, as we look with accuracy at who we are in our natural state we are deeply flawed both physically and spiritually.

At fifty years of age I know that my body is well past its peak. More broadly, creation itself is teetering as natural disasters invade and disrupt our peaceful lives. And then, even our souls and desires are twisted, for just like in Eden, we long for that which is not ours to have. Our instinct is:

- to keep and not share,
- to be angry and not calm,
- to be sexually perverse and not pure,
- to be liars and not honest,
- to be prideful and not humble,
- to be lazy and not hardworking,
- to be idolaters and not worshippers of God.

What is more, even though we are ruined, we think we are not! We are naturally impressed with ourselves and quite blind to how far the tentacles of sin have reached into our lives. In other words, it is our sinfulness that thwarts us from seeing our sinfulness. It is all shrouded because the eyes that we look through and the heart that we feel with are spoiled.

As we have said already, Jesus will only be our treasure and the one that we flee to, if we are able to see who it is that we are. As Dane Ortlund reminds us...

> we take a painkiller and go to sleep when we think we have a headache; we undergo chemotherapy when we know we have a brain tumour. The severity of our condition dictates the depth and seriousness of the medicine we know we need.[3]

Who I am, and who you truly are, is not defined by your success in relationships, your family name, the savings you've accrued, or even your attendance at church. Rather, your identity is bound up in what God thinks and what God sees. It is what He finds when the mask is removed and the stark realities of your heart are exposed.

When we think rightly and honestly about ourselves we will have come to an understanding of what Jesus was meaning when He looked at the crowds amassed on a hillside one day and lovingly He told them, 'Blessed are the poor in spirit for theirs is the kingdom of heaven' (Matt. 5:3). What was He saying? He wasn't scolding them or trampling all over their self-esteem. Rather, here was a Saviour who was revealing The Way. And *The Way* would firstly take them down. That is, only those who sink down

3 Ortlund, D. *Deeper: Real Change for Real Sinners* (Crossway, 2021), 40.

to see the true poverty of their lives will ever rise upwards into the home of God. This is the economy of Heaven. He wants us to be humbled as we see the mire into which we have sunk, and in seeing it, to long for a Saviour who reaches out and pulls us up into His arms.

Martin Luther understood this well. He wrote the following so we could think as we ought;

> God has assuredly promised his grace to the humble, that is, to those who lament and despair of themselves. But no man can be thoroughly humbled until he knows that his salvation is utterly beyond his powers, devices, endeavours, will, and works, and depends entirely on the choice, will and work of another, namely, of God alone. For as long as he is persuaded that he himself can do even the least thing toward his salvation, he retains some self-confidence and does not despair of himself, and therefore he is not humbled before God, but presumes that there is – or at least hopes or desires that there may be – some place, time, and work for him, by which he may at length attain to salvation. But when a man has no doubt that everything depends on the will of God, then he completely despairs of himself and chooses nothing for himself, but waits for God to work; and then he has come close to grace.[4]

Pride is always lurking. It follows us through life, fashioning us into arrogant and brash characters who know nothing of the lowly-suffering Jesus; the Jesus who hung in humiliation as if He were a sinner. There is no conceit at the cross for Jesus knows that God's wrath is just. It is deserved. It must fall. And yet sometimes as

---

4 Luther, M. *The Bondage of the Will* (Independently Published, 2021), 16.

sinners we miss this and, in the place of humility we bound along in life with no understanding of the terrible place in which we stand.

Here then is how the Bible defines me in my unbelieving state. We may feel we know ourselves but listen to what God thinks and dwell here. It will be good for you to be reminded of the reality of your condition:

- I am asleep (Eph. 5:14)
- I am akin to a lost sheep that is wandering and can't find its way home (Matt. 18:10-14)
- I am a stranger to God (Col. 1:21-23)
- I am unrighteous (Rom. 3:10)
- I am on the way that leads to destruction (Matt. 7:13)
- I am building my life on shaky foundations Matt. 7:24-27)
- I am following the ways of the world (Eph. 2:2)
- I am blind (2 Cor. 4:4)
- I am in a body that is wasting away like an old tent (2 Cor. 4:16)
- I am under God's wrath (John 3:36)
- I am dead (Eph. 2:1)

What is more, I am unable to raise myself up from either my physical or spiritual death and am therefore completely dependent on the intervention of Another. Without His intervention I will leave this world one day and face the justice that must come on my sin...and then there will be a third death. For after my spiritual death and my physical death I will arrive at the destination to which my way of life has led me, and hell will be my eternal home.

This is how we must think, for this is who we are.

Chapter Four

A Great Exchange

'But when the set time had fully come, God sent His Son'

Galatians 4:4

Responding to rejection and abuse is tough and often it reveals much about our inner corruption and how terribly drenched we are in sin. For most of us (or maybe I am just baring my own heart here) the deeper the abuse the deeper the urge to get even. Missiles are met with missiles. Bombs with bombs. Anger with anger. Hate with hate. Do we not desperately need the teaching of Jesus to His followers to 'turn the other cheek' (Matthew 5:39) for our natural impulses are spiteful when we feel slighted? In our natural sinful state we often need no convincing that it is normal to strike; to gain vengeance; to abhor; to abuse the abuser. Indeed, so tarnished are our hearts that secretly we will delight when our enemies suffer. Again the words of Jesus expose us in Matthew 5:44: 'love your enemies, and pray for those who persecute you.' Such compassion is shocking to us. Jesus' Kingdom feels all upside down.

We hear the news of a terrible calamity that our adversary has experienced and a smugness descends. We quietly smile!

Either that or of course we simply retreat from 'these people' and distance ourselves, vowing never again to get close. We will be better off without them. We are better than them!

In the narrative of the gospel we may well expect to find that God is the same. Surely He who has been spurned by His world will respond in kind and simply unleash His furious wrath on His enemies. We would think that the remaining dire chapters of humanity's story will find us all hopeless and cowering in the face of divine ire. A tsunami of anger awaits us with nowhere to run or hide. Or perhaps this God will wipe us out and start over. It only took 6 days the first time so might this not be His course of action? To begin again and set the world's coordinates in such a way that this time the same catastrophe which has befallen us will never be repeated? Or maybe He might simply back away from us and leave us to further descend into our pit of despair, laughing at our futility and finding pleasure in our pain? This would be normal to us. When hurt has come we usually choose to walk away.

I want to be clear in this chapter about a doctrine that often is strangely missing in modern Christianity. Namely, God does have wrath. He really does. Not the wild sinful fury of a human provoked but the settled wrath of a God opposed to sin. We should be thankful and glad that this is the case. That He *is* just. And that He *is* holy. God is not passive. There is no winking at sin and no turning away from the horrors we have become. Not once in Scripture do we find the carpets of Heaven being lifted as the human condition is brushed underneath. In the same way we are satisfied when the judicial system performs as it should, so we ought to be satisfied that God performs as *He* should. This is Paul's point when he tells the Romans that God 'will repay each one according to what he has done' (Rom. 2:6-8). Do we want that kind of God? Of course we do! Or at least we should. One who insists that justice prevails. We want the Hitlers to pay in the end. We want the sword of justice to fall.

But the problem is that sin is not only out there. It isn't merely in the headlines. Nor is it simply in the rascals of society who mug old ladies and steal cars. Rather, it is inside us, flowing out from us, infecting every part of who we are and what we do. The problem is that this is *our* problem. We should not need anyone to persuade us of our sinfulness for surely our consciences are seared and we can see our depravity. The sadness of being in the way of this world, as I have discovered, is that we remember the road we have come down. We recall many of our sins as if they were committed last night. They remain vivid and we replay them. A song or a place can spark a memory that reminds us of what we said or did.

The story of the prodigal son that Jesus tells in Luke 15 reveals the deep stain of sin that resides within every human being. We know, as the Rolling Stones do, that we 'can't get no satisfaction' and nor, it seems, can the prodigal. He has tried to silence the ache inside but he can't. It continues to speak to him. The unrest grows louder. He has gone as far away as possible to slake his thirst but his conscience will not be muffled and eventually, as he sits in the pigsty (a metaphor for our broken empty world) he knows that there must be a '*new way*.' Of course, in the language of our world this means new behaviour. It means trying new things and pulling our socks up. It would entail new habits, hobbies, diets etc. But that is because we have failed to see that our problem isn't behavioural; it is moral. It is not external; it is internal. We are alienated from God and flawed.

All this means that at the heart of the gospel there stands this fundamental question; what will this God now do with His wrath...toward me? Towards His enemy? How will He treat me? Like the prodigal in the story who vows to head back to the father he left, we await the dire consequences. We expect that a flood of abuse will come our way. And yet...

Enemy Love

...remarkably and uniquely, God loves His enemies. We need to let that settle deep down into our spiritual pores and drink in the countercultural Being who Scripture is revealing to us. Just when we least expect it, we discover that He loves us. The father's arms in Luke 15 are open to the pig-smelling prodigal, and so are God's arms open to you. Indeed, His purpose is broader and deeper than love. It is redemption, the buying back, and the bringing home of those who have despised Him, so that the relationships of Eden can once again be restored. He longs for nearness. To be at one again. If we thought that God was through with His world then we have misjudged Him and assumed He would be like our own vindictive selves. That's what the son in Luke 15 thought. He would maybe be a slave at best, and he would take that. He would crawl before his father on his hands and knees and beg for some kind of leniency and whatever substandard existence the father afforded him would be just fine. It would be his just deserts. But then he discovered that his father was not like him. He wasn't done with his son. The Father isn't through with you either. And at the heart of this mission to redeem is the sending of the Son that He loved so that on Him all your sins might be laid.

I love the hymn that John Newton published in 1779.[1] Perhaps in his day as in ours the name of Jesus was what was uttered when the hammer missed the nail and hit a finger. But Newton loved this name. He cherished it for it brought him to his Saviour...

How sweet the Name of Jesus sounds,
in a believer's ear.
It soothes his sorrows, heals his wounds,
and drives away his fears.
It makes the wounded spirit whole,
and calms the troubled breast.
'Tis manna to the hungry soul,
and to the weary rest.

It may seem strange to say it but the coming of Jesus is the event to which the entirety of the Bible builds. As Sally Lloyd-Jones tells us, "every story whispers His Name."[2] Every page. Every character. I wonder have you ever read the Bible through that lens? Jesus is not just offering a Gospel. Jesus *is* the Gospel. If 'gospel' literally means 'good news' then there is no greater news than Jesus for sinful rebels. Perhaps what we need more than anything is to climb inside the good news again to marinade ourselves in its life-giving message.

---

1 Newton, J. "How sweet the name of Jesus sounds." Originally published in 1621 Hymnals. 1799.

2 Lloyd-Jones, S. *The Jesus Story Book Bible*. Zondervan, 2007.

The Heart of Jesus

The Jesus who emerges in the Gospels is a Jesus who is compelled by love for the broken world in which He now walks. He is drawn to the distraught, the diseased, and the dying. He is not detached, or distant, or cold. Rather His life discloses that His heart is warm. He is affectionate, compassionate and accessible. If Jesus reveals to us the heart of God (John 14:9) as He claims, then the heart of God is not what we imagined. We have miscalculated Him on a mammoth scale.

- As He traversed across the region, 'He saw the crowds, and He had compassion on them for they were harassed and helpless, like sheep without a shepherd' (Matt. 9:36). In seeing He acts. He can't help it. He is drawn in to their suffering and sorrow. It is His natural reflex to meet the weary and to get under the load. There is an affection that leaks out of Him wherever He goes.

- Consider that Jesus was nicknamed, 'the friend of sinners (Luke 7:34). There were times when Jesus went to the homes of those who were loathed for their lifestyle was repugnant. They were untouchables and their sins almost unmentionable. And yet it is to them that Jesus is drawn, often spending the evening with them and breaking bread over a meal. He is pulled like a magnet into their company, not simply so that He can discharge His ministry duties but because He is the sinners' 'friend'.

- The tears of Jesus in John 11:35 not only provide us with the Bible's shortest verse but a window

> into the chords of love which bound His heart to Jerusalem. He stares over the city and the sorrow of others induce His own sorrow. He is deeply moved. We said earlier that we can find joy in our enemy's discomfort and tragedy. But Jesus is not from our world. He is not in our mould. His heart breaks and compassion tumbles out. He sees the mess and havoc that sin has brought into families, marriages, bodies, communities and in seeing it His tear ducts spill open.

C. H. Spurgeon, the great English preacher who himself was known for His own love of people, presented this Christ to His own congregation: -

> Jesus was constantly moved with compassion; for he felt all the griefs of mankind in himself. He took our sicknesses and carried our sorrows: he proved himself a true brother, with quick, human sensibilities. A tear brought a tear into his eye; a cry made him pause to ask what help he could render. So generous was his soul, that he gave all he had for the help of those that had not. The fox had its hole, and the bird its nest, but he had no dwelling-place.[3]

I want you not just to hear this loving Jesus, or to see Him in action, but to feel the love that cascades from your creator to you. To watch us distantly is one thing. To take on flesh is another. But to then embrace us, and ache over the human condition is beautiful. Time and again we read that Jesus is "moved with compassion". The lives of the blind, the lame, the bleeding, the prostitutes, the helpless,

---

3 Spurgeon, C. H. *The Compassion of Jesus* (Selected Christian Literature, 2018), 2.

the wicked, the outcasts, the bereaved and the dead are graced with His presence. He affords them His time and He enters into their suffering. And all this is done as the Father's representative. God is being disclosed and we discover His beauty is unfathomable. Jesus has come on His mission and in Him the love of God is on display. It is this Jesus, this same distance-closing Jesus, who beckons us to Him today.

The Work of Jesus

And then there is more. So much more to see and understand as we come to the cross of Christ where salvation's drama unfolds. As we said earlier in this book, it would be life-altering for all of us if we could see the wonders of creation afresh as if we were staring at trees and flowers for the first time. And now similarly, as we stop and gaze at a crucifixion where our creator bows His head, it would perhaps blow away much of our apathy and lethargic worship, if we could see this suffering Jesus anew.

Here now is where *The Way* opens up to us. It is here that the gate to Heaven swings wide on its hinges and sinners begin to travel upwards to the new world. We may believe there is a God, and even concede that He made us. And we might even espouse that we are depraved and lay the cause of this world's decay at our own door. But unless we make our way to the cross and there embrace Jesus, and see that He alone has made atonement for our sins, then we will always remain as we are.

I cringe when I think of my sins. There are so many I couldn't recount them all. Can you imagine the size of the book you could write on your own fallenness? Think of the chapter divisions alone! I live in a perpetual state of fallenness as we all do and so everything is tainted, even our best deeds. If I shared the mountain of failures that have marked me, I would be forever ashamed. I would probably lose friends as well. How then is it possible to be reconciled to God and escape the wrath that is due? Isn't this the great conundrum? The prodigal may well long for a fresh start and a renewed relationship. But how? And what of ourselves? We hear Paul saying in 2 Cor. 5:19 that 'God was in Christ *reconciling* the world to Himself'. But how can God and sinner be reconciled if justice must fall?

Paul waits just two more verses to tell us; 'He [God] made Him (Christ) who knew no sin to be sin for us, that we might become the righteousness of God in Him' [2 Cor. 5:21]. Here are the grounds of our reconciliation.

Exchange

It is important to grasp that in the Bible the word 'reconciliation' carries with it the idea of 'making a change' or 'exchanging'. If you went to the market, opened your purse, and handed over your hard-earned money, you were exchanging it for something that the vendor had. And this is precisely what God is doing. He is offering an exchange so that your reconciliation with Him can be secured. Jesus will take your sin. Indeed, He will become sin. He will be *made* sin, becoming the locus for all the Father's wrath. And in exchange, as you give Him your sin, He will cover you with His righteousness.

Sinclair Ferguson beautifully packages all of this for us in this sense: 'Jesus Christ, who knew no sin, became sin. We, who knew no righteousness, become, in Christ, the righteousness of God.'[4]

---

4 Ferguson, S. *By Grace Alone: How the Grace of God Amazes Me* (Reformation Trust, 2010), xiii.

Isn't this astounding to you? Do you not see what it is that God is extending to us? Not only will He declare us innocent (as He declares His Son guilty) but He will go further. He will treat us as righteous; as those on whom wrath must not fall. Here is God not ignoring our sins but placing them all on the Son He adores. It is Jesus who will carry them, just like the transfer that took place in Old Testament offerings. In those days the sinner would come before the priest and, while confessing all of his wrongdoing, hands were placed on the head of an animal as a picture of transferred guilt. The animal was now considered the sin-bearer. It had 'become' sin. And then it was offered up, vividly portraying to the forgiven man that to be reconciled was deeply costly. It literally required an execution so that he could be free. This now is Paul's message to every sinner that lives in the aftermath of the cross. The Lamb of God has been offered and executed. If we will come to Him He will take our place so that God can reconcile His enemies to Himself.

The Returning Prodigal

There is a wonderful line in the prodigal's story that always grabs me when I hear it. The boy had run and partied hard but he found a profound emptiness in it all. There was nothing that lasted and nothing that placated the desires of his heart and finally he is friendless, despairing and broken. And then the line comes. Jesus who is telling the story says that, '*when he had come to his senses*' (Luke 15:17) he resolved to return to his father.

What a wonderful moment! His conscience was screaming and his mind was settled. He would go back. He had to. There was nothing else that made sense. He knew that whatever his dad did with him, it would be better than where he now found himself. Even being a slave would feel like promotion compared to his destitution. As he makes for home and rehearses his grovelling 'I am sorry' speech he has no idea what awaits. How could he? He rounds the final few corners and walks to the gate of the family home and there is his father. He has been waiting all along. He is coming towards him, running, smiling, welcoming...loving. The father isn't vindictive. He is glad. 'My boy has come home!'

Perhaps now as you read this you are coming to your senses. After a period of lukewarmness and spiritual drifting you now know that you need your Father. You have tried this world but it is empty and minus the soul-satisfying union that God extends. Or perhaps, for the very first time, you are being pulled to your Maker. You know He is real, and you know that He calls. You must go to Him, with all of your sinfulness, and find that his heart also pulsates with reconciling, redeeming love. The prodigal left his father and lived in mess, and so did God's Son Jesus. He left Heaven's splendour for our streets. Born in a manger and with no place to lay His head (Luke 9:58).

Here is the gate through which we pass. Jesus quite literally is The Way.

Part Two

Keeping Going

Exploring how the journey continues

I have started well on countless occasions. Diets come to mind. So do fitness drives that have involved goals to run marathons. I once even started to learn Spanish in my spare time and I think I have four words now. It didn't last! If January is a month that sees many great beginnings, we might say that February is a month that brings many sudden ends. There is an excitement that comes when we set off on a journey and even more excitement when we reach our destination but, usually, in the middle our emotions tail off. Few of us enjoy travelling. It is tedious and laborious. Often there are long periods when nothing of note seems to happen at all and sometimes there is every reason to abandon the journey altogether and head back to the comforts of home.

It is with this in mind that we now need to address the struggle that the Christian life has become for so many. If we were sold a life that was akin to a Mediterranean cruise when we started on The Way with Jesus, we have gradually discovered how wide of the mark that was. It may have sounded catchy and appealing, as if we were signing on to a country club membership, but it has become clear what an outrageous lie we were presented with. The cruise has not materialised but the force 10 gale has. We now know that this spiritual journey is arduous. We also know that words like perseverance, endurance, resolve, and resilience are perhaps more helpful and closer to what is required from everyone who is making their way to the new world. God has not chosen to zap Christians out of their present surroundings (John 17:15). If He had done that then straight after becoming Christians we would have been ushered into Heaven with no time-lapse at all. We would have been *there* for years but we have now been *here* for years. Despite knowing where we are going it is possible we are tired and feeling very far from the goal.

I have known many new 'Christians' who seemed to start very well. They really did. I have been present when they said that they had trusted in Jesus, and often I have been there as they were baptised as well. But sadly, I have also watched as some have abruptly or progressively stopped living for Jesus. In some cases it was imperceptible at first but over time there are always telltale signs:

- a loss of joy in their lives,
- a decline in church attendance,
- a lack of love for fellow Christians,
- a growing embittered spirit in response to a tragedy in life,
- an unhelpful interest in the world.

I have also seen the older generation look over their shoulders and talk of those that they once journeyed with, prayed with, and sang with and yet now they will tell you with sadness that these people are not there anymore. They were travelling right at their side and in some cases were a tremendous means of encouragement to others and yet tragically they went back.

John Bunyan depicts this in his famous allegory of the Christian life when 'Christian' meets 'Pliable" close to the start of their journey:

> they drew near to a very miry slough [filthy quagmire] that was in the middle of the plain. And not watching where they were going, they both suddenly fell into the bog. The name of the Slough was Despond. Here therefore they wallowed for some time, being shamefully bedaubed with the dirt; and Christian, because of the burden that was on his back, began to sink into the mire. Then Pliable spoke:
>
> PLIABLE: Ah, neighbour Christian, where are you now?
>
> CHRISTIAN: To be sure, I do not know.
>
> PLIABLE: (Offended and angry) Is this the happiness you have told me about as we have travelled? If we have such a halting [crippling] disaster at this early stage, then what may we expect from now on till the end of our journey? If I escape out of this with my life, you shall possess the brave country alone for me.
>
> Hence Pliable, making several toilsome attempts, eventually struggled out of the mire on that side of the

> Slough which was closest to his own house. So he went back and Christian saw him no more.[1]

What precisely happens in all these instances of retreat will vary from one to the next. There is no set formula and our enemy, who we will meet more of in the coming pages, is not predictable. My theology tells me that God keeps to the very end all those who have come to Christ for forgiveness of sins, and so there must be a question mark that hangs over the profession of faith of those who retreat. Only the Lord truly knows what is in the heart and we must be content to leave it there. There are no half-saved Christians. Only those who are saved. Totally.

However, what I do know from personal experience is that there are tough seasons for every follower of Jesus Christ, and often they come not too long into the journey. I don't think anyone really escapes and makes it through without scars. I was a member of a running club as a teenager and the jostling in the races only served to add to the soreness that enveloped you as the race ended. There would be elbows in the ribs and spikes on your shins whilst on the track. It was harsh and pretty brutal and there was every reason just to drop out and let the others jog ahead. Enduring sounds hard, and it is.

Back in 1992 Alistair Begg preached a sermon on spiritual endurance and referenced a true story that first appeared in S. D. Gordon's classic, '*Quiet Talks with World Winners*'.[2] There was a group heading off to climb Mont Blanc in Switzerland and prior to departure they received

---

1 Bunyan, J. *Pilgrim's Progress* (Reformation Press, 1999), 46.

2 Begg, A. Sermon, March 18th 1992 "Climbing on Track'. S. D. Gordon, *Quiet Talks with World Winners* (New York: A. C. Armstrong and Son, 1908), 52–54.

final instructions from the Swiss guide who would lead the trek. He got the group in the room, and said, "Listen, let me tell you something. If you are going to make the top of this mountain you can only bring the absolute essential kit along and everything else must be left. Show up with your boots, show up with your ropes, show up with your ice axe, and don't show up with anything else."

A young Englishman in the group announced to the guide that, having heard the rules, he was going to do it his way. And he had already put together all the things that he was taking with him to the top. He had decided that his kit would include camera equipment, extra fluids, large bars of chocolate, blocks of cheese and blankets, because he liked to sit down every so often on the journey. The guide, unable to dissuade him, told the guy, 'You're out of here. You come under my rules, or you don't come at all. Goodnight.' The Englishman went away in a huff, and the guide turned to the group, and he said, 'Let me tell you, nobody ever makes the top of Mont Blanc carrying all that stuff.'

So they set off the following day—the Englishman ahead of them, the group with the guide following on. And as they make their ascent, they start discovering all sorts of discarded kit—blankets, cheese, old bottles, camera lenses, and everything else. Finally they reached the summit, and there was the Englishman with just the essentials – his clothes, boots, pickaxe and ropes. And S. D. Gordon, who first told this story made this observation:

> 'So it is in the Christian life. Many find that when they cannot make the summit with all that they hold in their hands, they ***let the summit go*** and pitch their tents in the plain. And the plain is so very full of tents.'

Here then is an enormous subtle danger for us. Starting well but not pressing on is common. Settling into spiritual mediocrity and trading Christian maturity for some of the world's 'kit' is what Satan holds out to the redeemed.

A Careful Balance

As we consider how we keep going in this journey it is vital that we pause right at the start and get our theological bearings. There is no question that we need to hold two clear Scriptural principles in perfect tension at this point and if we don't, we will quickly veer off and find ourselves deeply confused. On countless occasions in my journey so far I have found myself focussing on one of these truths while missing the other, and the result has been a very unhealthy spiritual season. In a sense it is like riding a horse. We will fall off if we lurch to either side and so there is only one place for us and that is right in the centre. Here then is what we need in equal measure:

> God will keep me to the end.
> I must run to the end.

Both of these statements are a summary of where this whole section is going and both of them are so tightly entwined that it is hard to consider them as separate thoughts. They come as a pair and must be pulled out of scripture at one and the same time. If we take them together we will see how the commitment of God is what fills us with the perseverance we need to keep going. If we take them apart, we will fall into dreadfully damaging snares that will slow our advance and hinder our spiritual progression. Some of us will know straight away what is dangerous here and we will delve into our memory verse bank to prove that something is not right. The problem is that, although we see the errors, we still live as if they were the truth. Our behaviour is not being driven by our beliefs. Here are the snares:

All God – No Me (God will keep me to the end)

On the one hand we may fall into the first of two extreme positions, believing that God will keep me and that, as such, I have nothing to do other than sit on my hands. I can perch myself on the back of the bus that is travelling to Heaven, take in the view, doze, and be a passenger, for God is up front and driving. He is making the effort and I'm just to sit tight and wait for the doors to open at the station. I play no part in the whole adventure other than getting on the bus in the first place. If He doesn't change me there is nothing I can do about that. Perhaps for some of us this is where we have strayed. For instance, how many times have we witnessed a Christian losing their temper and then, in their defence, heard them saying, 'This is just who I am. I am hot-headed. I speak my mind. You have to take me as you find me.'

That of course is a devastating fallacy and yet often it pervades the Christian population resulting in malnourished and immature disciples. If we adopt the '**all God – no me**' approach we will leave all our spiritual progression to God and never tend to the sin that springs up in our lives. We will not strive for godliness by forsaking the things for which Christ has suffered because we are on the bus and God is driving. That is for Him to sort out. That is what He does. Of course there is a whole lot of truth here but the problem is that our part has disappeared and we have erased the urgings of Paul to 'press on towards the goal to win the prize'

(Phil. 3:14). There is serious effort in that verse as we strain every sinew in order to gain ground.

I have often reflected on the pictures that Paul used to depict our Christian journey when he wrote to a young pastor. There is no mention of sitting on buses or lying on beach towels but there are references to soldiers who fight, athletes who run, and farmers who rise before anyone else and work hard. Indeed, these farmers know full well that unless the effort is put in the crops will not grow and the harvest will not come. By contrast the **'all God – no me'** approach will make me lazy and rather accepting of my shallow spiritual condition. We may not teach it but we have slid into its clutches and we're stuck.

This is the **All God – No Me** approach. If God doesn't do it then don't expect me to.

All Me – No God (I must run to the end)

By contrast there is another miscalculation that lies in wait to entangle us; namely, that my entrance into Heaven is hinging on me. We will say that God saves me but from then on it's up to my own grit and determination to hang on and push through. It's almost as if He has wound me up like a clock at the start and then departed, leaving me to tick by myself. If this is where we are in our thinking we will no doubt be feeling crushed by the weight of our eternal destiny. We rejoice that our sins are forgiven but we worry that we might botch things from here on in.

Sadly when we go solo and adopt the **'all me – no God'** approach we are signing up for a lifetime of doubt. If my entrance into Heaven is standing or falling on the attainments of a flawed sinner like me then how will I feel when I fall into a period of lust or greed? What will I conclude then? Or perhaps my quiet times will dry up and my worship of God will lack the fervency of previous years and what will I think about my heavenly prospects? Moreover, how will I view my ability to succeed in living out the experience of those who Jesus speaks about, who 'overcome' and get to gain an inheritance (Rev. 3:21)?

From experience I can tell you that such a person will dissolve into a puddle of uncertainty, always wondering if they will do enough in the end to make it the whole way. They are propelling themselves, like the Flintstones in their engineless car, and lacking the fuel to go the distance, fuel that comes from knowing it is God who saves. I don't just mean a God that saved in the past but I mean a God who goes on saving me from sin in the present and saves me completely in the future, to such an extent, that He guarantees He will finish what He started (Philippians 1:6). All of that comfort and assurance will disappear like water down a plughole when we err at this point. We will see the sin in our lives and the endless struggles to make any progress and our minds will be awash with concerns:

Will I get there?

What does God think of me?

What if I'm not good enough?

Here then is the Biblical model of endurance that Paul pulls together for the Philippian Christians.

> Therefore, my dear friends, as you have always obeyed—not only in my presence, but now much more in my absence—continue to work out your salvation with fear and trembling, for it is God who works in you to will and to act in order to fulfil his good purpose. (Phil. 2:12- 13)

This is not '**All God No Me**'. Nor is it '**All me and No God**'. Rather it is '**All God and All Me**.' I am involved in my own endurance. Notice the two central phrases that hold our doctrine in place at this point:

... 'continue to work'... 'for it is God who works'. This is critically important to understand and get right. To be clear this is not a call for any of us to earn our salvation for that is the work of Christ and Christ alone. 'He has appeared once for all at the culmination of the ages to do away with sin ***by the sacrifice of himself***' (Hebrews 9:26). Christ has accomplished our entire salvation. Every last one of our sins are dealt with and even our future glorification is secure. We will get to Heaven. It is certain. If you have trusted in Christ then you will reach the end point of the journey and delight, face to face, in your Saviour forever.

What then is the 'working' that Paul is calling for? Indeed, whatever this work is, we should notice that this is long-haul work for he urges that we 'continue to work', continually forging ahead, sustaining our efforts to the last. As we have said above, this is not salvation's work for that is finished. We are speaking about sanctification's work; that is, the work of becoming holy and like our Saviour from the point we become Christians until we stand at Heaven's door. We are called to 'work out our salvation' and yearn for the holy things that God treasures and longs to see in His children, and yet we are not working alone 'for it is God who works in you.'

Here are the grounds of our motivation: that God is doing the same work; that this also is His aim. He of course could do it all by Himself but out of sheer grace He has given you a piece of the action, a place in the workforce. You are to join Him and work at His side.

Paul's intention is to propel you on by stressing that He is holding you. He Himself shares the same purpose and the Holy Spirit who is in you will bring it to pass. You should keep going for God will ensure that the end will be reached.

Proof

What is at stake here is proof. If we are looking for verifiable evidence that we have passed from death to life and are on The Way to Heaven, then you will find it if you are working in tandem with God. This is the 'work' that is in view in Philippians 2 and it is this that we turn to now. My desire is to spur you on and graciously shout in your ear to keep going. To beckon you forward and urge you to recover from missteps and falls. Such experiences are familiar to every child of God.

Again what we need is a sight of Jesus who 'endured the cross' because of 'the joy set before Him'. It was the triumph of glory in Heaven that called Him. May it call you too.

Chapter Five

Every Day

The habits we need on The Way

'Since we have been justified through faith, we have peace with God'

Romans 5:1

Groundhog Day is celebrated annually on 2nd February in North America, the date that the groundhog apparently pokes its head out from its long winter hibernation. Much more broadly the phrase has taken on its own popular colloquial expression, due to the 1993 movie by the same name. In it Bill Murray stars as a weatherman who gets up each morning to find that the day's events are precisely the same as the ones he has just lived through yesterday. Every incidental detail mirrors what has gone before. Nothing is new. Like the hibernating groundhog he is stuck in a cycle of sameness, living life on repeat, unable to escape from its cookie cutter pattern. 'Groundhog Day' has come to mean monotony, repetition, and predictable humdrum living.

In many respects we may feel that we are living through yet another 'Groundhog Day' as we read this. Life is not full of memorable adventures, or at least mine has not been so far. There are past highlights that stand alone, and future events that we eagerly anticipate, but on the whole most of our days are hard to distinguish from others. They are bland. We don't rise in the morning expecting to be surprised. The average human lifespan is 27,373 days and the vast majority of those are filled with routines that are decades old. We sleep, eat, travel, work and then do it all over again. There is a lot of tedium. Our Thursdays are the same as our Tuesdays and we often yearn for newness. A craving for change that breaks the mould. Restlessness can come to us as we stare at the familiar and we long for that which we have not yet experienced to spice up our otherwise dull lives.

As we come to think of the mechanics of spiritual endurance I want to invite you to a 'Groundhog Day' that you need to excitedly embrace from conversion to the grave; namely, a daily return to the saving work of Jesus in your life. Your temptation will be to move on from it, but you must resist all of those urges and view them as an error of judgment that will ultimately derail you. Returning here as Christians must be our staple every day. Our meat and drink. Our all. In our quest for joy it would be easy to feel, now that we have started on The Way, that the cross is the past and we need to make our way to fresh future pleasures. There is a tendency in all of us to think like this. That we have been to the cross and 'done it' so to speak. That's how we began, but moving on needs something extra. We have ticked it off, understood what happened there, and now in order to grow and keep our spiritual momentum, we must discover what is next. As if there are deeper joys on the other side of the cross. Bigger truths. More thrilling experiences that will unleash within me the satisfaction I am missing.

As I say, there is a propensity in all of us to think this way. After all, many of us have grown up in gospel-loving homes and if there is one part of our faith that we think we know well it would surely be what Jesus has accomplished. We feel we have plumbed the depths of the cross and explored every conceivable nook and cranny. We may not be able to articulate all the nuts and bolts of our theology of Church or the Second Coming or the Trinity but we know what we are talking about at Calvary. In time we can start to think that journeying with God is about journeying away from there. We may even think that the cross is just milk and the meat course is deeper theology (1 Cor. 3:2). I have come to see that danger in my own life and so, in many respects, I am writing here into my Christian experience. And yet here is what I have come to understand. Christian endurance requires fuel. The right fuel. The healthy kind that sustains. And there is only one fuel that keeps a Christian running hard; it is remembering every single day that his or her justification has been an act of sheer great grace.

Dane Ortlund has taught me this more than any other author I know. In his book, 'Deeper', he puts it this way:

> It is common in some quarters of the church to think that the message of the gospel initiates us into the Christian life, and then we move on to other strategies when it comes to growing in Christ. This is a fundamental mistake. We will never grow truly as long as we retain this error. The gospel is not a hotel to pass through but a home to live in. Not only a gateway into the Christian life but the pathway of the Christian life. Not jumper

> cables to get the Christian life started but an engine to keep the Christian life going.[1]

When we are travelling on any journey it would seem odd if we suddenly rounded a corner and found ourselves at the very place we set off from several hours ago. And yet this Groundhog experience is our greatest need. We must not only start here but stay here and make this the place where we live. The cross is what sustains every ensuing step.

We are justified by grace

When we became Christians we were justified, that is, declared to be righteous by God through no merit of our own. Even though the Bible explicitly teaches that we are desperately unrighteous (Rom. 3:10), incredibly we have not been treated as our sins have deserved. That reality has a wow factor about it and we must fight to make sure it astounds us for the rest of our lives. We must never get used to it. Instead of condemnation we have exchanged our sinfulness for the righteousness that Christ possesses and we now find ourselves being viewed as the innocent party. Jesus has been made sin and we are viewed as righteous. This is what justification is.

It is important to note here that we have not been 'made' righteous for that is what happens in the ongoing work of sanctification; a lifelong Holy Spirit project as we are changed. We are still very much unrighteous and our families know it. So we have not *become* righteous but we have been *declared* righteous. That is how God views us. We who were prisoners to our own guilt have been brought before the Judge and told we are free to leave.

1 Ortlund, D. *Deeper: Real Change for Real Sinners* (Crossway, 2021), 17.

Of course this whole experience is the very antithesis of what is celebrated in our culture where earning is everything. We have, because we pay. We earn the right to drive by passing a test. Or we earn the right to practise medicine by succeeding in exams. We have done something and we have received what we deserve in return. This is society's way, and it makes sense to us. If a man is handed a 15-year prison term and he completes his sentence right down to the last day then he has earned his freedom. It is his right. He can walk through the prison gates and not feel he is in debt to a single soul in this world. He has paid his dues.

Here then is the very heart of our struggle. We haven't paid, and we never will. We never could. Not even a single penny. With our whole being, from now until the end of our journey, we will intuitively battle to lean entirely on a gospel that is wholly free and so at virtually every turn we will subtly try to add our own contributions. Of course, we never say this but it is there in our thoughts. We believe that our good days are adding more fuel to the fire of justification. By contrast our bad days are dowsing it in water. We are more loved when our lives are on track. And we are less loved when they are not. We are definitely on 'The Way' when our devotions are wonderful, but we have crippling doubts when a season of spiritual dryness arrives. This is why we need to keep coming back to the start. We must! Anything less will leave us clinging hopelessly to the wrong anchor. We must behold the suffering Saviour every day as He Himself makes the payment for the entirety of sins for us. And we must see the exchange; my sin to Him and His righteousness to me.

The Grace of Groundhog Day

There are many hurdles to Christian endurance. Satan is wily and he has his subtle ways of impeding our race. To that end, consider the following four that stand in our way and how this critical Groundhog experience will enable us to successfully overcome them all.

1. There are people talking about me

For many of us the opinions of others are suffocating. The advent of social media has given the whole world a voice and now we feel the burden to impress. We are longing for praise. It has become like a drug to us. If we get some it will propel us along for a few more days and keep us afloat. But if we get their criticisms and barbs, damage to our self-esteem will swiftly follow. Sadly our churches can be a hotbed for the sharing of opinions and we so easily get crushed. And what comes from all of this is usually deeply damaging in the long term, for many of us start to believe what our critics are saying (or not saying). We hang on their words, or we misinterpret their silence. In the end we view ourselves in the light of what we are hearing and often our sense of worth drops right through the floor.

By contrast, how different would every day of our lives be if we were able to see ourselves through the eyes of a loving Father? Would this not be transformative for many of us? Would this 'Groundhog' experience not enable us to keep travelling? To keep moving forwards in the knowledge that the pronouncements of critics are as nothing when compared with the pronouncement of God.

We spend our lives hanging on every word that drips from those who feel an urge to share their views. But imagine we hung on God's words. That they were our drug. A drug that we craved and ran to every day. Can you even begin to envisage the change if we started each day by rediscovering afresh that we are His justified child. Would this not be liberating for us? I'm not suggesting that we don't care about the opinions of those around us, for often our critics have truth to share, and words of reproach that we need. But what I am suggesting is that we must not allow ourselves to be defined by anything other than the definition that God gives. We need His perspective. It is His judgement alone that matters and He has declared it in the greatest court of all. Christ's righteousness is yours.

This is stunning in the extreme when we turn to Psalm 139 and recall that this God 'knows me'. He scrutinises my insides, inspecting every single corner of my life. There is nothing that is hidden from His gaze. 'Even before a word is on my tongue you know it completely, O Lord.' David reaches the only conclusion that makes sense, 'such knowledge is too wonderful for me.' Well of course it is. This is humanity completely revealed. And yet consider what it is that your justification reveals. God has seen who you are and you have no secrets. You are utterly exposed. Who you are in your inner being has been laid bare and observed, in the same way as a scientist examines magnified objects on a Petri dish. He knows more than your critics ever will. He has seen it all. And yet, because of Jesus, you have obtained a glorious righteousness and this all-knowing God accepts you.

When you know that you are loved irrespective of how you have performed, on that day you will be the most secure Christian in the whole world.

2. There's a past that still haunts me

For many of us it's not really the voice of others that inhibits our growth. It's our own. Our conscience speaks louder than anyone else that we know. The fact that all our friends have a past is often not comforting for we truly believe that our past is the worst of all. If they knew of it we would hide in a corner. Some of us would relocate. We have secrets that we have buried and tried to forget and, such is our shame we have never shared them with anyone. The more you grow into Christ the darker your sins will appear. It should be that way. He will appear lovelier and they will appear more depraved than you ever realised.

However, once again, let me urge you to hold the gospel before your eyes and see again what it is that your justification has brought. Your sins were placed on Jesus Christ. All of them. Even the ones that keep you awake at night. He carried them all away, and He did it so that your burden could be unstrapped from your back. He has carried it so that you don't need to. As a pastor I obviously know that this is the gospel, and yet I would be the first to say that it is still hard to think this way. To feel it. To press into it. To truly embrace these Jesus-purchased blessings at the deepest level of my soul. It makes more sense just to keep feeling unforgivable and dirty. To wallow and accept that my freedom in Christ will just have to be less than what others experience. And yet that is precisely why we need to keep returning here for we need to be systematically broken down by the power of the cross. Jesus has paid it all!

3. There's a sin that's too big for me

Thirdly, if we thought that coming to Jesus would mean we would never wrestle with sin again, we now know otherwise. We may have been declared righteous but we have still to be made righteous and that process is going to be littered with backward steps. Many of them. For some of us reading this there are secret sins that we have tried to conquer but they continue to rear their head. We feel inept and we can't shake them. The Devil has a foothold and we are distraught about that. The struggle remains as real as ever.

Can I suggest to you that once again it is our justification that acts as the engine in our sanctification. What we need most when we are in the trenches with sin is to see Christ. To see Him dying for us. To witness His suffering. A stern word may be helpful but not half as much as a dying Lord. A loving Lord. One who was willing to place His life in the hands of barbarous humans so that your Judge might declare you to be righteous. That is what will break our hearts, and call us on to further victories. Will we not press on for such a Saviour? Would we not find Him more appealing than the sins that call us?

4. There's an underwhelming future for me.

Lastly, we turn to the future. We may find obstacles to endurance in our past and present but looming large in our horizons is the spectre of ageing, decline and a rather underwhelming end – death! When we pause to consider that, we may start to wonder if it is worth it. For the vast majority of us this is the lingering question that slows us. If we knew for sure that the future was bright we would knuckle down, press on, and surrender ourselves more fully to the sanctifying work of the Holy Spirit. But sometimes we wonder. We have doubts. We're not sure if our sin will end up barring us from Heaven. Has Jesus saved us enough? We're not sure what the future will look like at all.

Yet again, in all of our fear, we must turn back to the cross and remember what it is that has been accomplished. Our salvation is total. When we ask the question, 'Did Jesus finish our salvation as He claimed from the cross', the answer is a resounding 'Yes!' It is done! It is not half-baked but fully baked. It is sin-conquering and grave-conquering. As Paul repeatedly tells us, we are so saved it is as if we are 'seated in the heavenly realms' already (Eph. 2:6).

I love how Don Carson spoke of this as he relayed his own father's passing:

> When he died there were no crowds outside the hospital, no editorial comments in the papers, no announcements on television, no mention in Parliament, no attention paid by the nation. In his hospital room there was no one by his bedside. There was only the quiet hiss of oxygen, vainly venting because he had stopped breathing and would never need it again.
>
> But on the other side all the trumpets sounded. Dad won entrance to the only throne room that matters, not because he was a good man or a great man – he was, after all, a most ordinary pastor – but because he was a forgiven man.[2]

2 Carson, D. *Memoirs of an Ordinary Pastor* (Crossway, 2008), 148.

We already have what we need

William Randolph Hearst was the Rupert Murdoch of his day, developing America's largest newspaper chain in the early 1900's. As his pastime he also collected antiques from all over the world, his money allowing him to amass countless treasures to fill his multiple homes. While reading an article on rare classics he saw a painting he was desperate to possess and so he summoned one of his staff to search for it. The cost in terms of money and time was irrelevant. It was a must. He had to have it. Whatever the outlay it would be worth paying so he could own it. Sometime later the man returned from his travels and came to see Hearst. He was glad to tell him he had located the painting. It had been hiding in his collection all along.

I want to end by echoing similar sentiments. You may be searching for something new. You have convinced yourself that there are spiritual treasures that you have not yet purchased. You are restless and you wonder if something is missing. And yet, all that you need is already yours. It's available for you. Best of all, you can take it out and stare at it every day and behold its beauty. There is nothing as valuable as the work of Christ. It is finished, perfect, and entirely sufficient. It is more valuable than you have ever realised. And all of it is yours. Go back there and see it. Remind yourself on a daily basis who it is that you are in Him, and what God has declared you to be. It is all that you need to endure.

Chapter Six

The Evil Day

Enduring through temptation on The Way

'Therefore put on the full armour of God, so that when the day of evil comes, you may be able to stand your ground, and after you have done everything, to stand.'

Ephesians 6:13

Isn't it refreshing when Christians are honest and real about their struggles? I know this can become excessive, when at times we choose to hang out our spiritual dirty laundry for all to see. I'm not sure that is always helpful, especially when there is instant forgiveness to be found in God. However, many of us spend our lives concealing all of our spiritual difficulties, whilst at the same time appreciating transparency in others. We want to see their flaws and vulnerabilities. It helps us to know that they have battles too. We just have more of an issue with them seeing ours, perhaps because we have convinced ourselves that no one could possibly find Christian growth quite as hard as we do. We've concluded therefore that it's best we pretend. We wear a mask, a mask of invincibility. We will keep saying we are fine, and then people will stop asking. Even more dangerous is the desire to keep up appearances, for fear that if other Christians knew the depth of our sins they would stop following us, or listening. As I say, all of this pretence in us is deeply peculiar given that we know what we appreciate in others; namely, Christians who let us into their lives and stand before us with complete authenticity. What we admire we are often not prepared to be.

Sometimes we miss words in the Bible that we would do well to mull over, and one of those words is found in Ephesians 6 when the Bible addresses head on the spiritual wrestling before us. It is such a small word that the vast majority of us will never have stopped to feed on the blessings that are to be found in it. Paul says, 'For our struggle is not against flesh and blood...' (Eph. 6:12). In case you missed it again, let me add some emphasis. He said, 'For OUR struggle...'. This is the Apostle Paul, one of the Bible's poster boys, and he is writing a letter that would be digested throughout history by millions of Christians all over the globe. His words would form part of the best-selling book of all time. This is not a personal letter. It is for public consumption. Families and members of the Ephesian church would ponder these sentences many times, discussing its contents and pausing at every detail. If ever there was a time to play to the gallery, hold out his credentials, and champion his spiritual superman costume then this was surely it. 'Your struggle' sounds better. We perhaps wouldn't have noticed the difference. I think had I been in his shoes I would have gone with that. He might even have spoken about 'the Church's struggle' and that would have kept himself at arm's length from the messy business of sin, temptation and Satan. At least no one would have known. But no! Paul doesn't do arm's-length Christianity. He doesn't want us to either. He knows we need each other. He may be 'in Christ' but he is also in the flames, and he is even willing to announce it. There are evil schemes to contend with, even for him.

With this in mind, as we sit in the company of an open and honest Apostle, it is vitally important for us to consider why it is that our Christian journey has not been a constant upward curve to this point. All of us would do well to give that question some time. We know that it is hard for there is clear proof in our own personal experience. Gaining spiritual inches has not been a comfortable process, and then retaining the traction we have experienced has been harder still. If someone were selling 'Instant Christian Growth Pills' we would sell our homes to get them for we long to progress.

The word 'struggle' in Ephesians 6:12 speaks of hand-to-hand combat, where our enemy is not distant but close up in our faces. He is near to us and deeply interested in derailing our journey. That Paul included himself in this battle is a sign that no one is immune. You too are being assailed and confronted by Satan himself, who seeks to place as many temptations and obstacles as he can along The Way. To be clear, Satan is unable to thwart your entrance into Heaven. That isn't what this war is about. He has lost on that front and he knows it. Everyone who begins on The Way will make it all *the way*. We often go awry at this point and think that there is at least a chance that Satan will succeed in reclaiming our souls and adding us once again to his ranks but that is why the doctrine of eternal security is so vital for us. We are the Lord's forever and He is ours. No matter what unfolds today, or what you do today, if you have embraced Christ you belong to Him. You are owned! Be convinced that nothing 'will be able to separate us from the love of God' (Romans 8:39). And be convinced that that truth sticks in Satan's throat.

The struggle, therefore, is not to arrive, but rather it is a struggle to mature as we go there. We are fighting for godliness and harvest. It is our growth that's at stake.

Our Enemy

If Paul was trying to play down the dangers that lie in wait for us all and glide over them quickly with not too much fuss, he clearly came up short when he wrote the eye-opening words of Ephesians 6:12.

> For our struggle is not against flesh and blood, but against the rulers, against the authorities, against the powers of this dark world and against the spiritual forces of evil in the heavenly realms.

The struggle that Paul is in, and we are in, is with evil personified. Rulers, authorities, powers, forces...a formidable who's who that is meant to jolt the Christian out of a peacetime slumber. Notice the layers in this verse and the multiple ways in which Paul fleshes out what we are facing. He labours over the enemy because he knows that most Christians don't. He takes time and spills ink, so that everyone concludes that this is serious and it isn't a joke. And yet many of us live as if this is trivia. Our lives often do not reflect that we are surrounded by dangers tailored to suit the weaknesses we possess. If we are in any doubt about that we just need to allow our eyes to climb to Ephesians 6:11 where we read we are facing '*the devil's schemes*'. That is, we are facing someone who is illusive, subtle, and deceptive in how he works. Indeed, his chief scheme is to convince us that this is a joke, for then he is at his most dangerous, and we at our most vulnerable.

Perhaps the most famous human scheme that springs to mind is the notorious Ponzi Scheme involving former NASDAQ chairman Bernie Madoff. A Ponzi Scheme takes investors' money and promises huge returns, and Madoff was responsible for the largest in history. Billions of dollars changed hands over the course of seventeen years until he pleaded guilty on 12th March 2009. His scheme promised the earth to customers. They signed up as believers, completely swayed by the promotional material that had been placed in their hands. They would give a little and receive a lot. What wasn't to like? It seemed like everyone would win in the end but, as with all schemes, they were being robbed in daylight and left empty-handed.

When temptation comes to you, it is this kind of scheme that is being played only the stakes are significantly higher than your bank balance. As we have said earlier, your growth into holiness is what Satan steals. If he can't change your destiny, he will go for the next best that's available and that is your harvest. When your day began this morning you may not have contemplated that this battle is ensuing, but that of course is part of the scheme. It is dangerous because it is covert.

Evil Day

We read earlier in Ephesians of 'evil days' (plural) which seems to be Paul's way of referring to the general state of the world we are living in. He informs us to 'make the most of every opportunity for the days are evil' (Eph.5:16). In other words, all our days are dangerous for there are distractions and pitfalls everywhere and we need to make sure that we learn to use our time well.

However, when we come to Ephesians 6:13 there is less of a general broad sweep of life in view. The lens has narrowed from days to one day; 'the day of evil.' That is, a particular day that dawns for every Christian as they journey with Christ. Paul is certain of this. He speaks of '*when* the day of evil comes.' We understand that every day is evil, for Satan is always busy, but here is a day that stands apart. It is unique. It is as if Satan's work has tapered down to a definite target. This is Paul's point. 'When the day of evil comes'...for you.

What then is this 'Evil Day?' How should we think of it? Perhaps the best way is to view it as having three constituent parts:-

- Opportunity
- Temptation
- Desire

Most days that we live are not marked by the presence of all three of these factors. For instance, today may well prove to be a day when temptation will arrive and we will hear Satan's voice calling us to deviate and run into sin. Despite this, the opportunity is not there to embrace it. We are perhaps hemmed in by family life, routines, meetings, illness, sports events, or even church. Satan may have called us but there is no easy route to it and so the temptation passes.

Moreover, today may be a day when there is an open door of opportunity before us. We have an evening to ourselves or perhaps we are travelling and have left behind the baggage of life for a few days. There is more disposable time. However, even with these opportunities we find that we have no desire. None at all. Rather, our desire is for faithfulness and for Christ to reign in our hearts. We love Him and love His ways. On this particular day we don't 'walk in the council of the wicked, or stand in the way of sinners, or sit in the seat of mockers' (Ps. 1:1). Rather we are delighting in the Lord. He is our all and we long to please Him by fleeing from the vile opportunities that have been presented.

However, at some point between now and Heaven all three of these ingredients will suddenly be there and we will know it. We will experience temptation. We will also find that the door of opportunity is ajar. And crucially, thirdly, we will want to walk through, allured by what we might find on the other side. We will hear Satan's voice and in our weakness we will be charmed – magnetised to what is being sold to us. When this is our situation and all three are present, we will know we have come to 'the evil day.' Sadly many wonderful Christians have fallen terribly on these occasions, often ruining their testimonies and ministries.

For some of us what we need to hear right now is that 'the Lord is gracious and compassionate, slow to anger and rich in love' (Psalm 145:8). We will be looking back from this vantage point with deep regret, guilt, and buckets of shame as we recall when Satan called us and we joined him. We were enchanted and we chose to follow the desires that had sprung up in our hearts and as soon as we tasted, we knew it was poison. I have often reflected on King David's life. If ever there was a man who honestly portrayed the blackness of his heart it was him.

> For I know my transgressions, and my sin is always before me. Against you, you only, have I sinned and done

> what is evil in your sight; so you are right in your verdict and justified when you judge. Surely I was sinful at birth, sinful from the time my mother conceived me (Ps. 51:3-6).

Yet another leader was led away. With perfect timing Satan preyed on David's weaknesses when a husband was away fighting wars (as David should have been) and a wife was needing to bathe. He too had come to 'the evil day'. He too was experiencing the incredible power of temptation. This is David remember. If it was a young Christian teenager we could understand (without condoning it). But this is a spiritual giant and he suddenly came tumbling down. And yet, wonderfully, he is in the Scriptures as an example of someone who lived to speak of the love of his God. David still had a future. God was not done with him:

> Blessed is the one whose transgressions are forgiven, whose sins are covered. Blessed is the one whose sin the Lord does not count against them .(Psalm 32:1-2).

When we are expecting nuclear judgement we find there is mercy that envelopes the confessor. We have offended the Father, yet His committed love remains the same.

Surviving

As we end this chapter there is another temptation facing us, namely, that we could become paralysed with fear as we consider the power that Satan continues to possess in this world. Indeed, we may look at David and a multitude of other Biblical characters and conclude that if these leading lights of the Faith were overcome then surely a certain inevitability surfaces regarding my own demise. More mature Christians than I have stumbled. Surely

I will follow! It's inevitable that my future will find me 'returning to my vomit' as Peter once so vividly put it (2 Pet. 2:22). And yet, what we must cling to is the hope that Jesus extends. The opening statement of our passage in Ephesians 6 does not simply say, 'Be strong!' Rather, it calls us to 'be strong...**in the Lord**.' To go there, hide there and live there; to make Him the strong tower that you run into.

There is nothing complex about any of this. There are no secrets that need unravelling. The Christian life is not about being strong and riding out the storms. The Scriptures never say to us that gritting our teeth and clinging on with white knuckles is the answer. Rather it is about a relationship with Someone else who is strong. It is about being led to 'the rock that is higher than I' (Ps. 61:2). A deep, daily, prayerful relationship. One where we are utterly dependent as we travel. We will come to this in subsequent chapters but what we need to understand here is that Christ, once again, is enough. We need Him and we have Him. He is the one who makes us strong for He is strong, and we are in Him. We are going to be assailed in this world but we can know what spiritual victory looks like as we go into battle behind our Captain.

Chapter Seven

Numbered Days

Recognising the brevity of The Way

'Teach us to number our days, that we might gain a heart of wisdom'

Psalm 90:12

I am writing this chapter while journeying to the USA and it will be a long day. I have a seven-hour flight to Toronto, a short train ride, two hours on a bus, a three kilometre walk in order to get over the Rainbow Bridge in Niagara Falls, and then a three hour road trip to Cleveland in a hire car. With layovers and waiting times I'm expecting it will be a full twenty-three hours before I finally rest again. The only consolation is knowing there is an end. I will get there. It is not forever. I will put my head on the pillow tonight, close my eyes, and wake up refreshed in the morning.

As journeying Christians it would be of immense help to us if we thought correctly about the length of our journey. The length of our time. The reality is that often we don't. We know that when a journey seems endless, despondency is near. We feel we will never get there and that this is too hard for us. However, in this chapter I want us to consider another danger that confronts us as Christians when we overinflate our allotted time and imagine we are guaranteed years before our end. This danger leads to indifference.

I'm reminded at this point of my first year at University which culminated in me failing every single exam. I thought there would be time to get serious with my studies. Nearer the exam date I would stop playing snooker and I would start reading books. A casualness had come over me and I drifted along. There was plenty of time to catch up, or so I thought! I would get focussed when I needed to and pull out all the stops, but until then I would have fun. I would hone my snooker skills in the process. Well, when the exam season came around the inevitable happened. It was too late. I had wasted a whole year and I had to live with the consequences.

Of course with exams there are always reruns, but with life there isn't. Those are the facts that we live with as we bring each day to a close. We have one go and then it's over and we will never be able to scroll back and relive what is already passed. As this same thought grips Moses' heart in Psalm 90 he feels he needs to return to school, sit under the tutelage of God, and gain the knowledge that he knows he lacks. 'Teach us', he cries. Here is a man who requires further education and the benefit of heavenly wisdom when it comes to the matter of his lifespan. He is ignorant and uninformed when it comes to time. 'Teach us', he says, 'to number our days'.

Heavenly Mathematics

Learning our numbers so we can start to count is one of the elementary developments that we delight to witness in our children. Before we can ever live life and make wise choices we need the rudiments of mathematics. Our finances depend on it as does our ability to tell the time. Children may use their fingers or an abacus. Adults may turn to calculators. Contractors have measuring tapes. Every time the aim is accuracy so the right answer is found.

When a Christian starts to total up his projected days on this earth there is a danger that his numbers are wildly excessive. Many of us look ahead and plan for the average life. 365 x 80 = our answer. Who needs an abacus when the sum of our time is as simplistic as this? And yet this Psalmist appreciates there is more to the equation. He needs to be taught to number his days aright, to count properly and make sure he is not dealing in averages. Indeed, when we apply heavenly wisdom the answer to that calculation is startling. We have just one. Today! There is nothing more that we can bank on. We cannot presume anything else. Were we to do that and look ahead, our equation becomes skewed. We are factoring in days that are not guaranteed. They are not here yet and they may never be here. As James so helpfully says to all of us, 'Why, you do not even know what will happen tomorrow. What is your life? You are a mist that appears for a little while and then vanishes. Instead, you ought to say, "If it is the Lord's will, we will live and do this or that"' (James 4:14, 15).

I still remember the day that a child from my primary school fell through a frozen river and died. I had been with him earlier that day and couldn't quite grapple with the news that suddenly unfolded later in the evening. He was gone, never to return. His life had been shorter than any of us had ever considered. However, even if our life is long it is still the mist that James describes. Whether fifteen years or eighty-five years, in the light of eternity it is a two second vapour that is there and then suddenly fades away. This is why heavenly mathematics is so important. As we journey on The Way we must think wisely about time, valuing it as a precious commodity that one day will be exhausted. We have it now but one day we won't.

The Wisdom we Need

As far as we know, this is the only Psalm that was written by Moses which, if true, makes it older than the rest by several centuries. And yet here is a lesson on time that every generation, including this current one, needs. Listen to how Moses frames it for us. He starts with this statement:

> Lord, you have been our dwelling place throughout all generations. (v1)

Christians have always been drawn to this verse because of the security that it paints for travelling saints. We love the idea that we are dwelling and resting in the safest place of all. God, it turns out, is not just who we go to. He is much more than that. Notice what Moses is saying. God is where we are. We hide and live in Him. He Himself is the place in which we dwell. As Paul said to the Athenians in Acts 17, 'God...is not far from any of us. For in Him we live and move and have our being' (v28). We can abide in Him and know the rest that this divine sanctuary brings. That is an invaluable image for all of us, as we journey in a spiritually hazardous world. Not even the devil can harm us when we dwell there.

However, as wonderful as all of this is, Moses is drawn here to something greater. There is an extra dimension that has caught his attention and he wants to share it. Look again at this opening verse:

> Lord, you have been our dwelling place **throughout all generations.** (v1)

In short, Moses is writing his Psalm of worship not simply to marvel at where we dwell, but to marvel at a God who has been precisely the same dwelling place for His people since the dawn of time. It is God's eternal unchangeableness that has overwhelmed Him. God has been God to successive generations, and they have all found Him to be unaltered. The God of Moses is entirely consistent with who you and I now know today. He is never in decline. There is no 'peak season' with Him which is followed by the ravages of age. Regression in any of His capacities is not what He knows.

Having stated this as the psalm's theme, Moses then proceeds to contrast this God who is unaffected by time, with those who are mortal and are limited by time. He continues by saying:

> Before the mountains were brought forth or ever you had formed the earth and the world, from everlasting to everlasting *you* are God.

That is a God who is eternally dependable and predictably perfect. And yet here is the contrast in the very next line:

> You return *man* to dust and say, "Return, to dust O sons of men."

The point is patently obvious to all of us. While God is everlasting, our lives are brief. We are marked with frailty and the best way to see it is to think more about God. We are, as he puts it, waiting on God to return us to our original material. Dust! Like new grass in the morning, he continues, which stands tall and vibrant, we become by the evening time 'dry and withered' (v6).' This is the wise perspective that the Bible provides and as much as we would prefer to banish our transience, we are not spared this harsh reality when we search the scriptures. My time is depicted as:

- 'a mist' that has such a short lifespan before it vanishes into thin air (James 4:14).
- being faster by far than a 'weaver's shuttle" (Job 7:6).
- being faster than a runner (Job 9:25).
- like an eagle that swoops down on her prey (Job 9:26).

As I write this I am nearing my fiftieth year on this earth. That doesn't bother me too much but what is much more arresting is that two decades from now I will be seventy years old and that is the age mentioned in v10: "The length of our days is seventy years – or eighty, if we have the strength". If you are also of a similar age to me, or even older, then you will immediately be lingering for a bit longer over those words. When I was younger and at school, the time it would take to get even close to seventy years seemed unfathomable. I would look at old people crossing the road and never even consider that one day I would possibly have the same crooked posture and withered facial expressions. And yet, as they say, 'time and tide wait for no man.' It all happens in the blink of an eye. And that is Moses' point.

History tells us that our forefathers have thought more deeply about these pressing matters than we have. We seem to want to separate ourselves from death. Apparently it's better by far to pretend it isn't coming. By contrast we are told that medieval scholars such as Jerome would often keep a human skull on a shelf so as to remind them of the brevity of life. Moreover, even in modern society until recent years, it was common for faithful churches to have a graveyard outside the church building, not simply so that burials were convenient but as a permanent reminder to congregants each Sunday that life on this earth is not forever.

Life is short. Eternity is long. Live like it!

How foolish then is the indifferent Christian! How out of place it is to be casual. Surely every spiritual wandering that takes place is due to a failure to treasure time. 'There is always tomorrow", we say. Or "there is always next year.' Maybe we are waiting for our education to finish before we get really serious with God and follow hard after the Lord Jesus. Or maybe when the kids have been raised and flown the nest we will finally sort out the spiritual malaise that often grips our devotional life. Then we will give our Lord the attention He deserves.

And yet what I have discovered is that while we wait for that perfect time of life, it simply never arrives. There is always something. There are always demands. There are always obstacles and multiple distractions that bar the way to maturity and endurance. Each phase of life has its own peculiar issues and in any case, as we have just observed, we are only guaranteed the phase that we are currently in.

A lady once asked the puritan preacher John Wesley how he would he spend his time if he knew that he would die at midnight the next day. He replied, 'Why, madam, just as I intend to spend it now. I would preach this evening at Gloucester, and again at five tomorrow morning; after that I would ride to Tewkesbury, preach in the afternoon, and meet the societies in the evening. I would then go to Martin's house...talk and pray with the family as usual, retire myself to my room at 10 o'clock, commend myself to my Heavenly Father, lie down to rest, and wake up in glory.'[1]

In other words, Wesley was a man who was numbering his days. He was making the most of time. I often wonder how much I would choose to change if, due to a medical diagnosis or knowing for sure the date of Christ's return, I was aware of the shortness of my days. If it were revealed to me that Jesus was returning next Tuesday I can think of many fixtures in my life that would suddenly be superfluous.

All is not lost

Knowing that time is limited and there are no reruns for any of us, Moses finally brings to us the lesson that we need as mortal beings:

> Teach us to number our days ***that* we may gain a heart of wisdom.**

In other words, if the first half of the verse is the Psalm's theme, then the second half is where we go from here. This is what numbering our days leads to. The upshot of accurate heavenly mathematics is that wisdom will grip us

1 J. B. Wakeley. *Anecdotes of the Wesleys* (Forgotten Books, 2018), 53.

and, not just in a light and passing sense, but in the very centre of our beings, our heart! We are to gain **a heart** of wisdom. Moses here is praying that all of our lives will be marked with the very mind of God, whether I am standing in the kitchen making endless dinners, or I am standing in the office with endless demands. When we have learned from God about time, we no longer speak of the "endless". Rather, we pray prayers along these kinds of lines:

'Lord, would you help me to be faithful today.'

'Lord, help me to remember that this is not forever.'

'Lord, would you constantly remind me to not put off what is urgent.'

'Lord, would you enable me to not presume on tomorrow.'

'Lord, help me to fix what is broken while I yet have time.'

'Lord help me to tell him about Jesus before you have taken me away.'

I love where this Psalm ultimately leads us. It's a wonderful reminder of the tender heart of an everlasting God towards his frail creatures and it's also what wise living consists of. Listen again to the heart of Moses as he grapples with his lifespan. How can a man whose time is short be glad? What can hold him and give him joyfulness? Indeed, how can we know any joy when death is casting its long dark shadow over us? Isn't it all just gloomy as we await our expected demise?

Well, not for Moses. And nor does it need to be that way for you.

> Satisfy us in the morning with your unfailing love, that we may sing for joy and be glad all of our days. (v14)

Beautiful! Here is where the withering grass finds its strength. Here is where the dust-bound find security. If you want to be wise with time, and have a joyfulness that not even the grave can steal, then begin each of your days ('in the morning') with a healthy helping of God. Be satisfied, says Moses, in this truth that, as He is unaltered by time, then so His love is unaltered. It will never fail. And that is worth singing for joy about, for all of our numbered days.

Chapter Eight

Better Days

Learning what is best for me on The Way

'Better is one day in your courts, than a thousand elsewhere'

Psalm 84:10

What is a great day for you? Think of all the occasions that have filled the last number of years. Which out of all of them rises to the top? Perhaps there was a holiday that still crops up in conversations at family gatherings. 'Do you remember the day when...?' Add in weddings, graduations, births etc. For us all there are showstopping moments in life, which evoke memories we will carry for the rest of our time here. No one would argue against seeing these days as particularly special gifts that Heaven showers upon us. Our lives can feel quite grey for large parts and then along comes an evening that brings a welcome splash of colour. We savour it and add it to our highlights reel.

With this in mind, imagine being able to have one day that is better by far than a thousand other ones combined. Now that would need to be a truly awesome day, right?

Twenty-four hours that are better than 24,000 hours! A thousand days is the best part of three full years. Think of all the events you could attend, and all the experiences available. You could fit in multiple holidays, play as much golf as you wanted, go on dozens of dates with your spouse and still have room for more adrenalin-filled evenings with your favourite pastimes. Would it really be possible then, to have just one humdinger of a day that was so satisfying it outstripped all of that put together? Is such an experience out there?

Well, the Sons of Korah seem to think so, and they are keen to share it with us. They have found it. The authors of Psalm 84 have placed life's opportunities in the scales and they have discovered what is 'better'. Better than all. Better than what the world will tell us is best. Better than what we are told is essential for our happiness. There is a way to spend a single day, they say, that leaves whole years of activity in the shade. Some of us at this point will be thinking of our highlights reel again, and we will be wondering what could possibly top the day when we paid off our mortgage, or when the job offer came through at just the right time, or even the year our team won the championship. What's better than that? What even comes close? Well, this is their assessment:

> Better is one day in your courts, than a thousand elsewhere. (Ps. 84:10)

Learning to Love the Presence of God

I want to admit something to you. Often I don't live as if the Sons of Korah have got it right. My guess is that you are the same. Worse still is this next admission – that sometimes I live as if I don't need a day with God at all. As if it's not essential, and as if it's not better. In fact, if you were to carefully watch how I spend my time I am sure there would be occasions when you would draw this conclusion: 'Graham thinks that just a single day of pleasure is way better than a thousand days with God!' How sinful we can be, even as Christians. There is a waywardness that can still afflict us after years of journeying to Heaven. What I want to argue in this chapter is that staying on The Way and keeping going over the long haul, is only possible when we are regularly and intentionally having the 'better by far' experience. Without God's company we are destined to struggle. We need to be with Him. And the wonder of the Bible's story is that we can be. God is not hiding. He is not illusive. As John Gillespie puts it, 'it is not as though we are brave explorers and God is some mythological land we are seeking to discover'.[1] Rather, He is inviting us daily to come to His courts and find that being there is more 'lovely' (Ps. 84:1) than anything else.

Psalm 84 is about knowing what is best for us, and then with all of our spiritual appetites peaked, going to take ownership of it. It is realising the value of God and concluding that, because nothing else compares, I must have Him. Listen to the Sons of Korah again:

> How lovely is your dwelling place, Lord Almighty! My soul yearns, even faints for the courts of the Lord; my heart and my flesh cry out for the living God. Even the sparrow has found a home, and the swallow a nest for herself, where she may have her young – a place near your altar, Lord Almighty, my King, and my God. (Ps. 84:1-3)

1 Gillespie, J. *Following Jesus in an Age of Quitters: The Resolutions of Jonathan Edwards for Today* (Christian Focus, 2024), 129.

Bird Watching

During the springtime we have excitedly watched as bird boxes in our garden become occupied with new tenants. There is usually a bit of a 'moving-in' process as the debris from the previous nests are tossed out. These new homeowners are fussy. Last season's furniture needs to go before they set about creating some pleasant surroundings for the coming weeks. Some twigs and leaves will be brought in. There is lots of industry and last-minute safety checks to ensure no predators are around. If all is well, and the coast is clear, it is time for the bird to 'dwell'. He or she is at home.

The authors of Psalm 84 have been birdwatching too, and they have noticed that some swallows have dared to build a nest, would you believe, right next to the altar of God. They have made their home there, quite possibly up in the eaves of the Tabernacle. Having scouted out all the trees and bushes available, they eventually plumped for a spot that places them, not next to a predator, but their Maker. Even the sparrow has done this, they say. Even little birds are in God's company!

The point is simple but truly profound. Learn from the swallows, follow their lead, and do the same. This is the call of Psalm 84. If it's possible for little birds then take up the opportunity as God's little children. Make your home where they have made theirs. Choose your resting place where they choose theirs. There will be other 'trees' and 'bushes' available. You can choose to find your rest with an X box controller in your hand, but there is also a prime spot that is available for you that is near to 'the Lord Almighty' (v3). You should take it.

The wisdom of the swallow has stirred something in the hearts of the Sons of Korah and now they reveal their desires; 'my heart and my flesh cry out for the living God'. This is the greatest pursuit of their lives. They long to be with Him. They want Him. Only He can fill the void, fuel their engines, and keep them advancing onwards. They have learned through the twists and turns of life that there are pleasures which offer much but disappoint, and then there is one Pleasure that always delivers. God is that pleasure! They write to us to tell us that exchanging your world-obsession for a God-obsession is possible.

Would You Rather...

Sometimes children will play a game called Would You Rather, in which two options are put before the participant. So...would you rather strawberry jam or raspberry jam? It can be as simple as that. Or, would you rather be freezing cold or roasting hot. In other words, two contrasting but straightforward choices.

Notice in this Psalm that the Sons of Korah have come to the crossroads of decision as well:

> Better is one day in your courts than a thousand elsewhere; **I would rather** be a doorkeeper in the house of my God than dwell in the tents of the wicked. (Ps. 84:10)

How wonderful! Do you see their hearts so clearly displayed here? And doesn't it immediately sound right to you? As if they have expressed what you also desire, but maybe have yet to practise. They would rather stand on the very fringes of the presence of God and take the lowliest task of holding the door keys, than be one of the gang who gets to sit in the warmth of the wicked man's tent. In other words, just a little of God is better than more of the world. They would take that every time.

Communion with God

When we talk of communion with God, we are talking of doing what the Father, Son, and Spirit, have been doing for the aeons of eternity within the Godhead. They have been enjoying each other, and dwelling together. They love each other. They are living together and experiencing that God is better by far. The beauty of the Gospel is that, now we have been reconciled to our God, we are invited to commune with Him too and experience the community that the Trinity enjoys.

Nevertheless, I want to assume that some of us reading this will be feeling a little ashamed as we listen to the Sons of Korah. We will love their devotion (and maybe we could preach great sermons about it), but we will be deeply envious of it. To this point in your life you have never been able to say that 'you would rather' the crumbs from God's table compared with a feast from the world. I'm not suggesting that you are filling your spiritual stomach with ungodly things but, I am suggesting that you are possibly not seeing God as 'better'. You are not savouring Him. You aren't able to say that your time with God today is actually the best part of the whole of today.

Spurgeon, the famous eighteenth-century preacher, once put it this way: 'has there not been sometimes this great temptation to do a great deal for Christ, but not to live a great deal with Christ'.[2] That's true, isn't it? Christians can have a hobby called church, whilst at the same time not be at home with Christ. Busy but not

---

2 Spurgeon, C. H. *The Spurgeon Series 1857 & 1858 Unabridged Sermons in Modern Language* (New Leaf Publishing Group, 2012), 119.

bowing. This is dangerous, for in time our stride will shorten, and our devotion will cool, unless we are being energised and fuelled by this 'better by far' relationship.

When we would not rather...

Having made the assumption that some of us are not quite like the Sons of Korah but want to be, let me close this chapter by speaking to you. Spiritual maturity takes time and God has not provided a microwave to speed up the process. Communion often comes from choosing. There will be days, praise God, when the feelings are there and you are able to say from your heart that you 'would rather be a doorkeeper in the house of the Lord' than have anything else in this world. Relish those days. They are special.

But then there will be other days when you choose God, without the feelings. You will have every reason in these moments to set your spiritual disciplines to the side and allow the opportunity to pass. Home life will intrude and that will be just the start. There is no question that busyness remains one of our biggest obstacles to dwelling near to the Almighty. Everything within you will say that you can get through the day without time with God. And that may be true – you may well get through it. The issue is, will you get through it whilst being near to Him? Will you get through it and say as the day ends that this was a 'better' day. A little of God, remember, is better than hours of scrolling. Minutes with Him is better than hours of sport. Learn that principle now, and carry it with you. An older saint told me recently that multiple ten-minute prayer slots throughout the day has become a new normal for him. Why not try that?

Every single saint since the story of grace began has communed with God in precisely the same way. There is nothing new for us here. It's the old, old story. I think there are three factors that will help us build our home with the swallows.

1. The Heart of God

John Owen writes this beautiful truth in his book on communion with God (by the same title): 'The greatest sorrow and burden you can lay on the Father, the greatest unkindness you can do to Him, is not to believe that He loves you.'[3] Just allow the richness of that thought to compel you to come today to your Father. The God that is waiting to commune with you, is the same God whose heart is full of love for you. He will not turn you away. He will not keep you at arm's length. You may not think that He loves you. You may not imagine, after all of the coldness with which you attend your devotions, that such a love would even be possible. And yet here is the truth – He does! And that fact on its own should woo you and call you to build your nest in the best place of all.

2. The Word of God

To know God, you must read and the Scriptures are where 'the Lord Almighty' is revealed. Because of that, the Scriptures are where your 'better' days are found. You will see Him in the mighty acts of Genesis. You will find Him in the stories of deliverance from Egypt. You will hear Him through the prophets. You will observe His wrath falling on all of His enemies. You will stare in wonder at this God in the manger. You will cover your eyes as He hangs in shame on a cross of wood. You will look again as

3 Owen, J. *Communion with God* (Banner of Truth, 2022), 12.

He emerges from death. You will see Him in power as the Spirit falls on the church and equips it for mission. And you will be gripped at the sight of this God in full victory as a returning Christ crushes all His foes underneath His feet.

You will not know these things, and savour them, if you are communing with Netflix. To build your nest there is to end up starved. Change your diet now or you will not have the spiritual sustenance to propel you forwards. Only the ones who are digging for treasure will find it. And so dig. Just like every other Christian who has lived near God has done. Choose to do it.

It is by reading the Scriptures we are set free from Satan: 'You will know the truth, and the truth will set you free (John 8:32).

It is by reading the Scriptures we will be sanctified (that is, become more like Christ): 'Sanctify them by the truth; your word is truth' (John 17:17).

It is by reading the Scriptures that Christian joy descends: 'His delight is in the law of the Lord, and on his law he meditates day and night' (Ps. 1:2).

It is by reading the Scriptures that we will keep going: 'Man does not live on bread alone, but by every word that proceeds from the mouth of God' (Matt. 4:4).

3. The Ear of God

Wherever you are right now, and whatever you are doing – you can talk to God. This would be 'better' for you. He is available. As Billy Graham says to us all: 'don't ever hesitate to take to God what is on your heart. He already knows it anyway, but He doesn't want you to bear its pain or celebrate its joys on your own.[4]

For some of us today the best prayer we could pray is a prayer of genuine repentance. We know we need renewal, and we know we need it now. Why not say that to Him. This is at the heart of communion; that all of the wreckage and dirt is removed so that nothing hinders our walk with God.

Is it really true that being with God for a short time is better by far than the best activities on the planet over a long time? It is true! Go to Him today. And then having done so, go to Him tomorrow. He is the best company as we stay on The Way.

All the way my Saviour leads me,
Cheers each winding path I tread,
Gives me grace for every trial,
Feeds me with the living bread.
Though my weary steps may falter,
And my soul athirst may be,
Gushing from the Rock before me,
Lo! a spring of joy I see.[5]

4 Graham, G and D. L. Toney. *Billy Graham in Quotes* (Thomas Nelson, 2011), 95.

5 Fanny Crosby, 1875.

Chapter Nine

Ordained Days

Suffering with hope on The Way

'All the days ordained for me were written in your book, before one of them came to be'

Psalm 139:16

'Embrace the chaos'. That was his advice for my life. I had just become a father of five (now six) and an older gentleman who had also walked in Abraham's shoes as a father of many, decided that I needed some counsel. Perhaps he saw the fear in my eyes and knew, without asking, that life was about to go up a few notches on the crazy busy scale. He took me to the side and this was the wisdom he had for me: 'Welcome the madness, hold your own plans loosely, and just embrace the fact that the future will be full of the unexpected'. I am still grateful he gave me his time.

There are few days that ever pan out in the way you envisage during those first few moments of semi-consciousness in the morning. Lying there in bed you had it all mapped out and the line from 'A' to 'B' was straight. 'This day will be fairly easy to chalk off', you said, and then with a precise diary tucked under your arm, you bounded off into the predictable. However, by the time you climb into bed later that evening you have passed through a number of conflicts between the children, taken some unexpected criticism at work, received a huge tax bill, and squeezed in a trip to A&E for good measure. Where did it all go wrong? And what happened to that straight line you saw so clearly from your pillow?

Perhaps you are reading this and wondering where it has all gone wrong for you. A day of unfulfilled plans is one thing, but a season of tragedy is another, often acting as a hinge on which the entirety of life swings. Being a pastor affords you a seat on the front row and sometimes the view is hard to take in. It is a beautiful privilege to walk through pain with fellow travellers and yet, even though grief is frequent, there is still a palpable shock when the news breaks. Someone in church has taken unwell. A sudden accident has claimed a life. An expecting mother has miscarried. As I write this I am expecting to hear soon that a dear believer in our church has been widowed. Since the fall in Eden this has been the disorder we've known. We make our plans but we hold them loosely for, as James records for us, 'you do not even know what will happen tomorrow' (James 4:14).

Sovereign in the Sadness

When David writes to inform us that every day is an 'ordained day' we are hearing a truth that is meant to plunge the Christian into a place of security. God is ordering all of my steps. He is in control. He is holding nothing loosely at all. As the kids' chorus reminds us, this Great Being has got the whole wide world in His hands. Moreover, every detail matters to Him. This is meant to be mind-blowingly wonderful for Christians who live in a world where even tomorrow is obscured. And yet maybe you are reading these words today and, as you do so, you are reflecting on a loss that has been so life-altering that your world doesn't feel held, but dropped. God dropped it! It WAS in His hands but then it slipped. I still remember when one of our children dropped an enormously sentimental piece of china and it shattered into hundreds of shards. The irreplaceable was now all over the floor. Broken beyond repair. Is that how you feel today? Someone who has yet to recover and you have long since reached the conclusion that perhaps you never will. You are grieving, and the grief is so deep that you are finding The Way a very difficult place to be.

Not long ago one of my friends took his own life. He had planned to do so and yet didn't tell me or anyone else. I think about it more and more as time passes and I wish with all my heart that God had ordained I would have been there that day. If only he had called. Or if only I was aware. I would have dropped everything and rushed to be with him. Other friends of mine have lost parents in the most painful of circumstances. Members in our church have lost children. And then there is your story where the inexplicable has suddenly unfolded. Perhaps friendships have been lost or a season of unemployment has come and you puzzle over the truth of God's sovereignty, struggling to marry it to your tears. How could God have written *THIS* down?

When bad things have suddenly erupted around us, it is tempting to want to let God off the hook. In other words, we naturally want to make the Bible fit around our circumstances as opposed to the other way around. As humans who are addicted to logic, we are quick to deny that God can be involved in tragedy, let alone be sovereign. It is easier and neater to speak about a broken world, perhaps echoing the sentiment that 'the devil did it' as we put all of our suffering down to his meddling with life here. The results are still equally as painful but at least we are spared the torture of factoring God into the equation. We want to see Him as not being a part of this. We don't have space in our logic to factor that kind of thinking in, for if He was involved then what kind of God must He be?

Many great Christians have wrestled with this, and so if you are in this place, take comfort in that. Millions of saints have stood where you are. The journey to Heaven is tear-soaked. There are vexed faces every way we look. Joni Eareckson Tada's diving accident in 1967 which left her a quadriplegic, was one such occasion when God's sovereignty and human tears collided. As far as she was concerned at the time, her whole life was ruined and she couldn't wrap her head around the references to God's total control over every day. If this was true of God then, why did He allow this? There is nothing sinful about asking the "why" questions of life. Please believe that God is able to take your questions. His shoulders are broad enough to bear the load of your confusion.

What Joni discovered and documented was this: that God permits all sorts of events to happen, and even the ones that He doesn't approve of.[1] For instance, she noted that in Lamentations 3:33 God 'does not willingly bring affliction or grief to anyone' and yet, four verses later in 3:37 we read these words:

---

1 Eareckson Tada, J. 'Who really controls the suffering you go through?' Published on Joni's Posts on joniandfriends.org. 7th October 2022.

> Who can speak and have it happen if the Lord has not decreed it?

In other words, in verse 33 God takes no pleasure in our grief. And yet in verse 37 He allows it and sends it as part of a bigger picture. There is mystery in there that finite brains will not fully untangle and so not all of our questions will be silenced here. However, there it is in black and white in Scripture that in a tragedy of inestimable proportions, our God can be loving and sovereign all at the same time. God does not get a kick out of our agony and, as a loving Father I am certain His heart breaks when His children are crushed. And yet Joni and countless others on The Way have discovered that God has sent the heavy burdens as part of a wider and often unseen picture.

The more I have encountered pain in my own life and seen it in the lives of others, the more I have wanted to work out what options we have to reach for. Consider with me the following three:

1. God has the ability to protect us from tragedy and tears, but doesn't want to.

If this is where we land in tragedy then we have got serious issues to work out as Christians. In this scenario we have a very powerful God who is totally able but thoroughly unwilling to act for our good and, I'm sorry – but who would want to love and serve Him? This is a ghastly thought, not too dissimilar from parents who are able to provide protection for their children and yet in an act of capriciousness, choose instead to heartlessly withhold it and watch as pain is faced.

A God that can, but doesn't! A God that could but won't. Sufficient for all of our needs, and yet unmoved and unwilling to get involved! The rest of scripture bars us from going here, and so don't go here. This is impossible for a God who, in Romans 8:28, is actively 'working' for the good of those who love Him. You can be sure today that your God is able and willing. He is both!

Another option is this:

2. God wants to protect us from tragedy, but sadly He doesn't have the ability to do so.

In this scenario we have a God who is much more palatable because His heart is not stained with detached emotions. He really does love us. We want Him to be like that. He views us as children whom He longs to keep from the dangers of the cliff edge. The problem, however, is that He can't. It seems that life is beyond Him. Whether due to the sheer number of children that He has to care for, or the unpredictable catastrophes that take even Him by surprise, He is just not able to be God to us all.

I urge you to search the scriptures to see if this kind of God is presented to you there. Do you see any inability in Genesis? Is He depicted as being inept and incompetent when the Red Sea needed to be parted, or when the walls of Jericho had to be shaken? Do you look on at the plight of humanity and observe that God just couldn't rescue us from the clutches of the Devil? Did God bungle it on the third day at the tomb of His Son? Again, when we come to tragedy we must conclude that a God who mismanages our lives is not a credible answer to the pain.

And so we come to this:

3. God has all the ability to protect us, but there are occasions when He desires to achieve something as part of His sovereign purposes that is greater than protecting us.

As hard as this may well be for some of us to truly accept, I offer this to you as the only answer that makes sense when pain has arrived.

If we go down the first route then we end up with a God who is aloof and cold. If it's the second, then my God is powerless and I am cast on the raging sea of life's chaos. But if I rest in the truth that God loves me and is fully sufficient, but on occasion will withhold His protection because His ways are not my ways (Isa. 55:8), then I can trust Him as I cry. You may discover His purpose in this life, but then again you may not, and not knowing will require great faith on your part. You will need to trust Him. But the wonderful discovery that the Bible brings to its readers is that you *can* trust God. The way that this works is that as you trust, He will hold. God drops nothing, and He certainly will never drop you.

As the old sailor John Newton once exclaimed: 'His love, in time past, forbids me to think He'll leave me at last in trouble to sink.'[2]

Staying on The Way

There are countless other stories I could share at this point where the notion of God ordaining all of our days has jarred with human experience. And yet all that matters as you hold this book is *your* story. The inexplicable has come to you and it has shattered the norms that you enjoyed as a

---

2 Newton, J. *Be Gone Unbelief* (Hymn 511).

family. Where do you go from here? How do you keep on the road that leads you to Heaven?

In times of suffering and tears, well-meaning pastors have tried to offer comfort to grieving saints by declaring that 'God didn't have anything to do with this trial that has come to you.' Such sentiments warm our hearts momentarily but they never last the test of time. Similar statements emerged in the aftermath of the attacks on the World Trade Centre in September 2001. A pastor on a radio program who was trying to make sense of the evil that unfolded declared that God wasn't involved and that 'Satan is still the prince of this world.'

Friend, I need to tell you something. God is involved. Moreover, God *did* and *does have* a connection with your suffering. That is hard to hear but there is hope for us in that.

In the Bible our God is sovereign over:

- the forces of nature (Ps. 147:15-18)
- plants and animals (Jonah 4:6; Matt. 10:29)
- apparently random events (Prov. 16:33; Acts 1:23-26)
- rulers and nations (Job 12:23-25)
- major disasters (Lam. 3:37-38; Amos 3:6)
- the spiritual forces of evil (1 Samuel 16:14; Matt. 8:31-32)

Consider with me, God is sovereign over that which is lesser to Him than you are as His child. So, be sure then that He is also reigning with love over you. To say otherwise is to remove the only hope that we have.

There is a tapestry that is being woven by God that has dark threads as well as golden ones and we need to convince ourselves, even when feelings scream otherwise, that all the colours of this tapestry are part of God's good plan. There are going to be seasons of doubt for you and the questions will pour from your heart. I honestly believe that is ok. Moreover, you will wonder if there is anyone else out there who really understands what it is you are going through. My intention in this chapter is not to wash away your pain but to give you an anchor in the middle of it. That anchor is a loving and sovereign God. He is both able and willing, but there are times when He will choose a way that is far removed from what we had hoped.

No matter what you are passing through right now, would you always remember that that's exactly what you are doing – you are *passing* through it! You will not always grieve and ache. Hope is beckoning you onwards. Heaven is before you. Jesus, who Himself, has been in this valley of tears, has made it home as the first fruits of all who will follow, and He will wipe away all of your tears.

Chapter Ten

The Lord's Day

Guarding every Seventh day on The Way

'I was in the Spirit on the Lord's Day...'

Revelation 1:10

Being a pastor brings many blessings. It can be hard, but it really is the best job in the world. Let me share with you what I am often most thankful for as time has passed; every week without fail, whether I feel the spiritual tingles or not, I am part of church life on a Sunday. The calling that God has placed on my life has meant that this one-day-in-seven rhythm is etched into my schedule. I am always there. My calling expects me to be. Most of you reading this will face a weekly decision, but pastors who want to retain their employment status don't. I get up on a Sunday and unless ill health thwarts me, I'm going! I think the Lord knew I would need that kind of rigid hedge around my life. I am thankful that not all of my attendance flows from fulfilling my contractual obligations. On the whole I have been 'glad when they said to me, let us go to the house of the Lord' (Ps. 122:1). But there have also been some Sundays when that has not been the case as life and sin has encroached. I have wished that I could opt out. Just for a week! I have hoped for excuses. The joy of the Lord perhaps hasn't been there or I simply got used to the gift that church is. Whatever the case I have gone, and in the end I have been abundantly blessed. Therefore...

> God, thank you for making me a pastor because, if You hadn't, I am so sinful I would have skipped dozens of Sundays to this point.

By contrast, no doubt you do have the luxury of choice come the first day of the week. Let me be blunt and to the point. I feel sorry for you. Every seventh day you may hear Satan's whispers and have to face a genuine decision. Do you go or not? Do you need to? Is it really all that necessary, and isn't there something called grace that covers even attendance indiscretions. Well there definitely is grace for you. All the grace you could ever need. Nevertheless, I am sure there have been decisions in relation to the Lord's Day over the years that you now regret. At the time you rationalised them but now you know the truth. Sunday came around and you chose not to go because...

You had a cold.
You were out late the night before.
You had a tough week ahead.
You had just had a row with your spouse.
You knew the preacher would be boring.
You wanted to watch the Cup Final on TV.
You were tired.
You needed 'space'.
You had to prepare for that presentation on Tuesday.

Instead of being in the one place that would help you inch forward on The Way – you caved. Dare I say it, you listened to the wrong voice. The choice was held out before you and as you listened to your feelings or were led by your circumstances, you removed yourself from the environment that God Himself created for you – Church! Covid of course, along with the advent of online services, has only served to increase the popularity of 'sofa church'. Why journey to a building and rub shoulders with those odd people who occasionally press your buttons, when you can sit in your favourite chair in your living room, clad in pyjamas with a latte in hand?

The term, 'the Lord's Day', only appears on one occasion in Scripture (Revelation 1:10) and given it is used with no explanation, we can assume that the first century believers were already familiar with the expression. They knew exactly what it was that the Apostle John meant. The Old Testament Sabbath ran from sunset on Friday to sunset on Saturday. By instituting it in Deuteronomy 5:15, God had called His people to pause. The rest of life would be hectic and so God knew a Sabbath was required during which they would remember how they had been delivered from Egypt. Everything else was set to the side so that minds were focussed and worship flowed. They needed to recall the past. They were never to forget the hole out of which they had been pulled.

When we come to the New Testament the concept of the 'Sabbath' was still in use in Jewish communities (Matthew 12:5; John 7:23) but as Christ's Kingdom is established it would be different deliverance that would come to the fore of the Christian's mind. This time it wasn't from Egypt. It was a greater deliverance. Because of Christ the powers of sin and death had been overcome. He had been laid lifeless in a sealed tomb, His body bearing the marks of the torment it had endured. But the grave could not hold Him. The Saviour had triumphed, and in His triumph He had set sinners free. As such it would be Sunday, the day of resurrection, that would now be guarded in the weekly calendar. It was another pause. They needed to recall the past. They were never to forget the hole out of which they had been pulled.

As B.B Warfield puts it;

> Christ took the Sabbath into the grave with Him and brought the Lord's Day out of the grave with him on the resurrection morn.[1]

The Lord's Day is called such because it was on this day of the week that the Lord rose in triumph. It was *His* day. Sunday is the Son's day. As those early Christians gathered, the tone was joyful and full of praise to the one who had inaugurated a new and lasting order. As Paul reveals in 2 Corinthians 5:17, it was on that first Sunday that the new creation itself began, for all those who are 'in Him' are now seen in that sense. Brand new creatures! Forever distinguished from the hopelessness of the past. Christ had started something on that first Sunday that would never be undone and every subsequent Sunday would prevent forgetfulness.

1 Warfield, B.B. An address delivered at the Fourteenth International Lord's Day Congress held in Oakland, California, July 27-August 1, 1915, published in Sunday the World's Rest Day. 1916, pp.63-81, and in The Free Presbyterian Magazine. Glasgow, 1918, pp. 316-319, 350-354, 378-383. Also as a pamphlet, Glasgow, 1918.

Should I stay or should I go?

I understand that relationships with others in the family of God are risky. It will always be that way and maybe as you read this you are nursing some relational bruises! Life with Christians who are flawed will be tough. I am sure others would say precisely the same about life with you. When you pack a bunch of sinners into the same family, throw in dozens of differences and temperaments, and then call them to regularly meet together – expect that you will encounter times you would rather be without. That is a polite way of saying there is jeopardy in church. It will disappoint at times and be more akin either to a morgue that needs to be revived or a boxing ring that needs calmed. If you are hoping that Church will be Heaven on earth then you are in for one almighty shock to your Christian system. Christians are broken and because Church is full of Christians you can be sure that Church will be a bumpy ride.

Even the early church discovered this just a few decades after Christ's resurrection. The Lord had only just left for glory and yet Euodia or Syntyche, two ladies in the church in Philippi, were struggling with 'loving one another' (John 13:34). That just about says it all, doesn't it? The Lord had laid down His life and portrayed His love for these women in the most staggering way of all, and yet they couldn't get their act together, set aside their differences, and take their cue from the lover of their souls. If they were here today they would tell you that being members in that Philippian church was hard.

And yet, be that as it may, there is something that is riskier by far to your spiritual journey than church attendance. Namely, non-church attendance. A recent survey revealed that 30-49 year old churchgoers are attending church far less frequently since Covid[2] and for the majority this is not due to health concerns. For some it's just no longer convenient.

I wonder what your attitude is to the Lord's Day. Do you see it as integral to life itself? Is it a must for you? Have you joined up the dots and realised that your spiritual progression on The Way, and the healthiness of your stride to Heaven, is directly linked to your commitment to Sunday worship? Or is it the case that you got slack? You used to be all in but not anymore. In all my years of pastoring I have never met a strong Christian who was flaky when it came to Sundays. Not one! Those that have endured and gone deep have also been present. They had deduced that Sundays nourish. They got out of their beds and they set off to get what they knew they needed.

Habits

Here is the sequence that we find in the New Testament:

- In Acts 2 the Spirit descended in power at Pentecost.
- The upshot of this experience was that in a short period of time the Christians had commenced meeting together regularly 'on the first day of the week' (Acts 20:7).
- By the time we get to Hebrews 10:25 there is a warning to 'not give up meeting together **as some are in the habit of doing.**'

2 Cox, D. A., J. Benz and L. Witt-Swanson, 'Faith after the Pandemic: How COVID 19 Changed American Religion' (American Religious Benchmark Survey, 2022), 10.

In other words in Acts 20 they had great habits but by Hebrews 10 they had developed some truly awful ones. They had started well but tapered off, forgetting what Sundays were for and why they were good. What they were now doing with their Sundays is not revealed but it is abundantly clear that they weren't doing what they should have been. The world had got it's clutches on to their schedules and quickly that one day had become the same as every day. In the years since, this sad sequence has often been repeated.

- Saved.
- Meeting Regularly.
- Regularly Missing.

If this is you, let me state the obvious. Christians need church. Finding a healthy one might be your challenge but we need to be there and in the middle of the family of God. And here's why.

1. We meet on a Sunday so we make it to the Final Day

It really is as serious as that!

Isn't this what is uppermost in the mind of the author of Hebrews? That we 'do not give up meeting together, as some are in the habit of doing, but we encourage one another – **and all the more as you see the Day approaching.**' Do you not hear the connection in those words between meeting and making it? In other words, Sundays are like links in a chain that hold us fast until the last day.

If you are converted as a fifteen-year-old and you live until you are eighty you will be afforded the privilege of well over 3300 Lord's Days. That is a staggering privilege. Keep in mind that the thief on the cross didn't get one! He never went to a church and never met with the people of God. Not one week in his life was marked with this bolstering experience. The truth is, he didn't need it. He was saved and then instantly he went home. But you need it. Maybe more that you realise.

Church is a 'means of grace' that channels encouragement into your soul. I'm not saying that your pastor will preach a home-run sermon every Sunday, but I am saying that faithful teaching, genuine fellowship, remembering the gospel, and being prayerful will fuel you up. It will keep you going. That's what the writer to the Hebrews had in mind back then, and given we are much closer to the last day now, 'how much more' should we commit to our gatherings. We need each other. Free-spirit Christians are not Biblical Christians. Get up and get out so you get to the end.

2. We meet on a Sunday to encourage others who are there

Have you ever considered this when you have reflected on a service and said, 'do you know, I didn't get much out of that today?' Getting something from church is important, but make no mistake that giving to church is very important too. Your attendance matters because others need you. Husbands, wives, aunties, friends, and children are all needing the same fuel that you need. Just like you, they have emerged from a week of trials and failures. In the light of that, listen again to the writer to the Hebrew right before he warns against not meeting together;

'And let us consider how we may spur one another on towards love and good deeds.'

There it is in black and white for us. Attendance is not just about you. Attendance is about you motivating others. And how do you intend to spur anyone on even a single step if you are three miles away perched on your sofa at home? In other words, by not attending you are saying in a non-verbal way that the spiritual vitality of others is not as important as your convenience. Get up and get out so that others get to the end.

3. We meet on a Sunday to reach those who will not be there

In one of the most famous statements that Christ has left us, we get this beautiful inside out theology laid out. Listen carefully to what He says:

> by this will all men know that you are my disciples when you love one another .(John 13:35)

Surely this is one of the greatest motivations to make sure you are there. By loving on the inside in church, Jesus is saying we will reach those on the outside of church. By revealing that a community of love is possible even when we are so different, we will be seen by the world to be followers of the Lord of love. Have we really grasped the heart of this? The church is not to come up with strategies to reach the lost. Rather, the church is the strategy. It is God's plan A. When we gather, love, and dwell together, Jesus assures us that this dynamic will be so other-worldly it will penetrate the darkness around us.

In a world that is often so loveless and cruel, the need is for the Lord's people to love so intentionally and beautifully that outsiders will see it, be captivated, and come inside. Get up and get out so that others get in.

4. We meet on a Sunday to be prepared for Heaven

If your church is functioning as it should then Jesus will be worshipped in songs, preaching and the sacraments. He is the Head of the church and from Him flows the very life of the body. Therefore, to be there is to be exposed to the very blessings that mould sinners over time. It's a transformative experience. Over the long haul we are remade so we gradually resemble citizens fit for Heaven itself. We will take on the family likeness as children of the Living God. Again, this will not be a radical change that happens on a single Sunday. Rather, it's the accumulative effect. Your own children are shaped over years and years, and so are God's offspring. Time is involved and lots of Sundays. I can assure you that someone who spends 3300 Lord's Days in church with an open heart will be more like Christ than someone who doesn't.

Therefore, guard this day! This is not a call to strict Sabbatarianism but it is a call to reject the 24/7 schedule of the world and make Sundays special. Your endurance depends on it.

Part Three

Arriving Home

Exploring where the journey leads

C. S. Lewis knew how to endure and draw from the hope of Heaven. We need to learn from him. The loss of his dear wife Joy in 1960 brought into his soul a pain that he would carry with him for the rest of his earthly days. 'The death of a beloved is an amputation', he wrote.[1] Joy had been at his side as his best friend since they married four years previous, but cancer had claimed her. She was gone now and their home felt empty. There were times he had thought his grief was abating, only to find that he was once again as heartbroken as he had ever been. 'Grief', he observed, 'is like a long valley, a winding valley where any bend may reveal a totally new landscape.'[2] It was to be for him a nightmare relived.

However slick the prosperity gospel proponents may be, the sound bites have no answer to this kind of sorrow. We are not promised health and wealth in this world, and most of us won't get it either. I'm sure you have discovered that by now. This valley of tears is going to intrude on our

1 Lewis, C. S. *A Grief Observed* (Faber and Faber, 2013), 60.

2 Ibid.

dreams and as much as we will want to escape, we will need to forge ahead and have a hope as Christians that can't be crushed. Just three short years after the passing of Joy, C. S. Lewis would disclose where this hope is found when he penned a letter on June 17, 1963. Mary Shelbourne, a friend, was gravely ill in hospital and Lewis was writing to encourage her. From all he had learned he was able to share this nugget of gold which successive generations of Christians have leaned on...

> There are better things ahead than any we leave behind.[3]

This statement has been a go-to for me as I have walked through this world. Starting on The Way is vital. So is continuing. But finishing and arriving at our destination is the ultimate goal. It is why we started in the first place. What Lewis believed about the future was exactly the same as what Paul himself would articulate when Caesar was holding his life in his hands. With his earthly days hanging by a slender thread he would declare that death would actually be 'gain' (Phil. 1:21) for him. Leaving here is a 'better' experience than staying here. Better even than any of the best times he had lived through here. The peak in his journey wasn't in the past. It was ahead!

Please observe at this point that the world does not believe this for a second. It is firmly of the view that our best life is now and what we have here is it. There will be nothing else beyond the horizon of our days; certainly nothing that will eclipse the joys this world affords. Just yesterday I read the sad story of a Dutch couple who chose duo-euthanasia because one of them had developed

---

3 Lewis, C. S. *The Collected Letters of C.S. Lewis Vol 3* (Harper One, 2010), 1430.

dementia.[4] Jan and Else had been married for almost five happy decades but, with no prospect of Heaven before them and believing that nothing 'better' was ahead, they concluded they had nothing to go on for. Even though Jan was perfectly healthy, Else had an uncertain future which meant that there would be no more 'gain'. They had lived, laughed and loved and now it was over. They simply went out for one last meal before dying together in a clinic.

That is the world view of unbelief and it is sad. It preaches that our joy graph will rise in this world before starting to flatline. By contrast, the world view of the Christian is that what is ahead is better than marriage. It is better than your best days as a mother. Better than winning. Better than all the empty offers of the world. Better even than your most euphoric experiences. It will indeed be 'gain'.

I wonder do you live with this reality regularly before you? Do you intentionally bring to mind that this world is not your home and that soon, whether it be when Christ returns or by your own death, you will be in the presence of God Himself? You will get more when you die than you ever had when you lived.

What does 'soon' mean?

I used to be deeply troubled by the 'soonness' of the return of Christ that the end of the Bible speaks about.

> He who testifies to these things says, 'Yes, I (Jesus) am coming soon. (Rev. 22:20)

---

4 https://www.bbc.co.uk/news/articles/c0jjq2vynq7o 'Dying together: Why a happily married couple decided to stop living' 29/6/24.

In my naivety as a younger believer I was sure that 'soon' would mean shortly after August 1983 when I first got to know the Lord. In fact, a few years later while travelling home late at night, there was an unusual shaft of light that burst through the darkness of the night sky. I was driving on my own and, as ridiculous as it seems now, I was convinced it was the Lord's return. What else could it be? Before I knew what I was doing I had pulled over, got out of my car, and knelt down in front of the headlights. I would soon be in Heaven! I was about to see Jesus and I was seriously excited! After a short period of time had passed I soon realised that it was, in fact, the moon and not the Lord. I sheepishly looked around to see if any curtains were twitching, dusted off my trousers, and climbed back into my little Peugeot.

Although these memories seem humorous to me now, I do feel that age has removed this sense of expectancy and excitement. I often live as if I am a resident of the world and not a sojourner to the next. As if all of my gains are here and not found in what is coming. Even writing this down unnerves me. To some extent, I can be found in the mould of Noah's neighbours who were consumed with life's affairs, and I am guessing there are times when you are too. We are so used to the predictable and the tangible that we can't imagine anything else – and certainly not anything else that is better. What could be better than the birth of your child? Or what could outstrip the fellowship that we get to share here as Christians? And yet here is the truth to which the whole of the Bible points; when the Lord comes or when He calls you, you are going to experience joy unparalleled and that thought is designed to be the greatest spiritual energy booster we have as believers.

For the joy set before you

If life has not panned out as you would have hoped, whether that be due to mental, physical or relational struggles, then please consider the prototype that Jesus is to you. As always, His example is perfect for weary travellers and so look to Him as His own suffering descends. He was human as we are, and in a body that knew pain as ours do. He was also headed to execution of the worst kind and He knew it. The cross had been casting its shadow over His entire earthly existence and yet now the 'time had come' (John 12:23) and Jesus would be required to endure. The question for Him and for all of us is simple. How do we keep going when present circumstances are excruciating and it feels like our world is collapsing? What motivation could there possibly be if the people and things that we treasure are being removed from us?

Here was our Lord standing on the cusp of torment unimagined. Moreover, prior to the cross...

He had been homeless (Matt. 8:20)

His family had thought He was crazy (Matt. 12:46; Mark 3:21; John 7:5)

He had faced temptation from the Devil (Luke 4:1-13)

He had lost His friend (John 11:1-45)

He endured gossip and slander (Matt. 12:24; John 6:52)

He endured extended periods of hunger (Mark 11:12ff)

He was constantly criticised for his ministry (John 5; Matt. 12)

He was mocked (pick a verse!!)

His message was rejected (pick a verse!!)

His disciples didn't understand Him (pick a verse!)

All of this was before the buffeting that the cross would bring but now with the cross, the suffering gauge would rise. He would be ripped from His family, betrayed by His friends, stripped, beaten, and even pronounced guilty by His Father for your sins and mine. No one came back from crucifixion. Everyone accepted there was no future beyond it. The only hope the crucified criminal had was that the suffering would eventually end. Death would win and the pain would recede (at least in this world). This was seemingly what lay ahead for the Lord. He had had His time and there was nothing 'better' to be tasted. The perfect Lamb of God was to become sin (2 Cor. 5:21) and bear the weight of the curse.

I am not lessening what you are walking through right now but I think I am on solid ground in saying that Jesus' load was greater by far. Therefore, how He endured is how you can too, and Hebrews shares the secret with us all. The author puts it this way;

> And let us run with perseverance the race marked out for us, fixing our eyes on Jesus, the pioneer and perfecter of faith. **For the joy set before him He endured the cross**, scorning its shame, and sat down at the right hand of the throne of God. Consider him who endured such opposition from sinners, so that you will not grow weary and lose heart. (Heb. 12:1-3)

Here, fellow travellers, is the engine that propels you to your destination. Jesus endured; '**for the joy set before Him**' and quite rightly we are told to 'consider' this. He made it all the way through the cross and the shame that went with it, only because He was able to see what lay beyond. He knew there was 'gain' and that was the hope that held Him in His darkest hours. From the cross He would see His weeping mother and that was a grievous loss to Him. Judas' betrayal for spare change was another blow that He surely carried on His mind. And then came His anguished cry of 'my God, my God, why have you forsaken me' (Matt. 27:46) as His precious eternal relationship with His Father was severed. His holy Father turned away. All of His past sufferings combined were as nothing when compared to this. Each were terrible experiences on their own but Jesus would carry them together as redemption was purchased.

What sustained Him? What held Him together and kept Him going? One reality! There was joy coming in His Father's presence. Heaven was near. He would go through the cross and on through the grave, and emerge on the other side. The cross was not the terminus. It was the journey to the terminus, and the terminus was Glory! Therefore, here's what Jesus knows and shares with us. He knows that joy is not found in popularity, for of course He didn't have any. Nor is it in acceptance, success, or money. Rather, it is found in the conviction that a new world packed full of everlasting joys is on the way. As others have observed, for those who do not have Christ, the transient joy of this world is the closest they'll ever be to Heaven. For the believer, this world's fleeting sorrow is the closest they'll ever be to hell.

As this book concludes I want to hold this before you. Christ is your model for endurance. Where you are going if you have Him as Saviour, is going to be unimaginably beautiful. Your Saviour knew that and it drove Him on. Lewis was the same. That just leaves you and me.

Have you forgotten that 'no eye has seen, no ear has heard, and no mind has conceived what God has prepared for those who love Him' (1 Cor. 2:9). In other words, even your best thoughts of Heaven have fallen short. You can't comprehend the flood of joy that will consume you when you first see it. It will all be better, and way beyond the current capacity you have to imagine.

I don't want to minimise your present losses, but I do want to maximise your future gains. I have watched on as a pastor when those who made professions of faith have wandered away. Where they are with the Lord I honestly don't know but I do know that 'he who endures to the end will be saved' (Matt. 24:13). What that means is this; making it to the end is part of proving the realness of the start. When the storms of life are beating down on us and unloading all sorts of heinous blows, we need to persevere. Jesus shows us that we can! Just as He did, we must believe that the best is always ahead and that no matter how bleak things are now, they'll get better by far. It's time we thought more about Heaven...

Chapter Eleven

The Way that lead to Life

'I write these things to you who believe in the name of the Son of God that you may know that you have eternal life.'

1 John 5:13

How many sermons have you heard about Heaven? I'm guessing the answer to that question is, not many! Fewer still will have been good ones. Bizarrely we seem to be terribly untaught regarding the place to which this entire Christian journey is heading. We know the name of our home but not much else besides. Is this not odd? Can you imagine choosing to emigrate to some far-flung part of the world without first exploring what life would be like there? Would it not be more normal to study this new land and pull together all of the available information? This, of course, is where your motivation to make it there would come from – knowing the glories of the world that awaited you.

With this in mind, how strange is it that the average Christian is vague on the New World. Moreover, our lack of teaching has also led to a chronic lack of accuracy. John Eldredge picked up on this when he noted the following:

> Nearly every Christian I have spoken with has some idea that eternity is an unending church service...We have settled on an image of the never-ending sing-along in the sky, one great hymn after another, forever and ever, amen. And our heart sinks. Forever and ever? That's it? That's the good news? And we sigh and feel guilty that we are not more 'spiritual'. We lose heart, and we run once more to the present to find what life we can.[1]

This places us in a terrible position; untaught, inaccurate, and as unclear as we can be about the prize that lies ahead. I have come to believe that at the heart of all of this is someone very sinister indeed, the devil himself. The father of lies has been sowing a lot of them regarding our destiny. That may sound over the top to some but the Bible itself bears this out. Having been removed by God and barred from ever entering Heaven again, it enrages him that 'lesser mortals' such as ourselves have been invited. He is missing out while we are brought in. For us the best is ahead but for him it's the worst. Therefore, it is hardly surprising that the great beast in Revelation 13:6:

> opened his mouth to blaspheme God, and to slander His Name and **His dwelling place** and those who live in Heaven.

Few verses in Scripture expose the heart of Satan quite like this one. Here is a Being who is consumed with a trinity of hatred: God, God's children, and crucially,

1 Elderidge, J. *The Journey of Desire: Searching for the Life We've Only Dreamed Of* (Blackstone, 2013), 111.

God's home. In other words, it's not so much that Satan's strategy is convincing the average Christian there is no Heaven. I have yet to hear that the Lord's people have imbibed that lie. Rather, his assault is on the nature and beauty of Heaven. Diminishing the prize that is coming will serve to suck the joy from our spiritual lungs in the present. And joyless Christians are precisely what Satan wants. If he can't get excited about Heaven then he doesn't want you to either. His best hope is making you question whether this journey of faith will be worth it in the end. The Land that is before us is meant to be what pulls us along the road, and not least when life is at its bleakest. Therefore, if Heaven is not all that glorious then that would be deeply damaging indeed. No joy. No perseverance. No true conviction that glory awaits.

When does eternal life begin?

Believing that eternal life is waiting for us when we open Heaven's door is surely one of the most common theological bloopers of all. Intuitively we believe that Heaven is where we get to taste it and in the here and now we are simply looking forward to it. We have to die first before we receive it. Perhaps the reason we think this way is because there are innumerable parts to our lives in this world that we do not want to be eternal. For instance, imagine living forever with that limp you developed in your early 40's. Or what about your current city being your eternal dwelling, and having to put up with the rat race of this world for time without end. For the Christian there is every reason to conclude that salvation's sequence is something like this:

Conversion – time between conversion and death – death – eternal life in Heaven.

It is for this reason that the Apostle John is at pains to stress something entirely different. He understands that human logic is a dangerous old thing that usually leads us down all sorts of wrong alleys. Note what it is that he is saying to these dear folks who read his epistle.

> I write these things to you who believe in the name of the Son of God that you may know that you **have** eternal life. (1 John 5:13)

Not that they are getting it, or that it is coming at some stage in their future experience. Rather, they possess it now. These people are still alive, still earth dwellers, still suffering, still ageing, and still have to face death. And yet the life which Jesus offers has already commenced. I can't help but feel a tremendous sense of security as I write those words. I *have* eternal life now. Would you let the transformative nature of your new-found status amaze you today? I'm sure you have all kinds of reasons to think that little has changed since you met Christ. Your suffering hasn't diminished. In fact, it's probably worse than others are aware of. You are still in that ageing body and you are still in this valley of tears with plenty of reasons to lurch towards despair. And yet the truth is that you are as secure in Christ this side of Heaven as you will be on the other side. Death is just another step.

How Long? How Good?

There are two parts to the life that Jesus gives:

- The first is quantity (how long?).
- The second is quality (how good?).

You should pause and reflect on that for a moment. Life with Christ is long. And life with Christ is really good – no matter what the devil may say. What we can deduce from John's words is that the quantity is given to us in full measure now, and the quality is only beginning. When we have Christ everything changes. 'I have come', said Jesus, 'that they may have life, and have it *to the full*.' (John 10:10) That fullness is ours now because we have the Son of God in our lives and what could be better than that? Life without Him is empty. Life with Him is brimming.

However, and this is vitally important to grasp, many of the rich blessings that flow from having Christ, such as the goodness that this will bring to our bodies, minds, souls, relationships, desires etc will only fully be known when we have reached the New World. We are 'groaning inwardly as we wait eagerly for our adoption to sonship, the redemption of our bodies' (Rom. 8:23).

Therefore, understand that the eternal life that is yours is not just offering a quantity of time (how long). If that were the case you would simply live forever with the depression that has afflicted you for years, or with the same propensity to sin that you were born with as one of Adam's offspring. Thank God that it is not only a quantity of time. He is also offering quality time (how good).

Where will I go when I die and what will it be like?

Should we leave this world before the Lord's return, as Christians we will exist in what is often referred to as the intermediate Heaven. That is, a place that God has created for Christians to live in as they wait for the second coming of Christ. Only when Christ has returned will we be led in to the new Heavens and Earth. Perhaps this intermediate state is a scary thought for you. Maybe you are thinking of family members who have already passed away and you wonder what life for them is currently like.

With this in mind I want to refer you to the passage below that is tremendously enlightening as we think of this intermediate Heaven.

> When he opened the fifth seal, I saw under the altar the souls of those who had been slain because of the word of God and the testimony they had maintained. They called out in a loud voice, "How long, Sovereign Lord, holy and true, until you judge the inhabitants of the earth and avenge our blood?" Then each of them was given a white robe, and they were told to wait a little longer, until the full number of their fellow servants, their brothers and sisters, were killed just as they had been. (Rev. 6:9-11)

As Randy Alcorn states,

> Unless there is some reason to believe that the realities of this passage (Revelation 6:9-11) apply *only* to one group of martyrs and to no one else in Heaven – and I see no such indication – then we should assume that what is true of them is also true of our loved ones already there, and will be true of us when we die.[2]

Therefore, learn the following (I am leaning heavily on Randy Alcorn's book on Heaven by the same title) regarding what happens to believers who die before Christ has come back.

1. When these people died and went to Heaven, they continued on as the same people who had been martyred

2 Alcorn, R. *Heaven* (Tyndale House, 2004), 67, emphasis original.

while on earth. In short this means that there was continuity between who they were here in this world and who they are now in the next world. This will also be true of you. You will not cease to exist when death comes.

2. Note also that these individuals were known for how they had lived in this world. They had 'been slain because of the word of God.' Even their testimony is remembered. Their earthly lives had not been eradicated. How they lived mattered much after death. It was celebrated. God had not missed their faithfulness. Again, this will be true in your experience.

It is clear from this passage that not only did God remember what had happened to these martyrs, but the martyrs themselves remember. They are clear that they were murdered for their faith. Often we conclude that post-death our memories will almost be wiped out and we will start afresh but this is not substantiated here. Our lives from this world, to some degree, will be remembered. This correlates with our ability to give an account for our lives to God (2 Cor. 5:10 and Matt. 12:36). Believing that all is forgotten when we die doesn't stand up to the scrutiny of these passages. Your journey will be recalled, and those details will help you to magnify the Lord Jesus even more than you would be able to if your memory was expunged.

3. When we read that 'they called out in a loud voice' there is, as a minimum, a suggestion of some kind of physical part to our experience in this intermediate Heaven. We struggle at this point to understand fully what this means because our bodies will still be in the ground waiting for the resurrection that Christ brings. However, when we are told that these saints have voices, white robes, and an ability to hear the voice of the Lord,

we can assume that there is some physicality to their existence. The same will surely be true of ourselves.

4. The fact that 'many' people were crying out in 'a loud voice' (singular) indicates that when we get to this intermediate Heaven we will have said goodbye to all disunity. Daily in this world there are many different perspectives. Many voices are sounding out views that are not in keeping with who God is. Church can lack focus at times. We can seem to be facing in a thousand directions. Not so in Heaven. We will all love the same things, voice the same things, and share the same outlook.

5. It is wonderful to learn that these people in Heaven are fully conscious. They are not sleeping or waiting under the influence of a celestial anaesthesia. They are aware of how things are in the world they have left, and they are very aware of each other and God. You will be too!

6. We also note that these people are able to ask God questions ('how long?'). Two realities spring from this:

- when we get to this intermediate Heaven we will not know everything. We deduce this from the fact that these martyrs have unanswered questions.

- there is a tremendous intimacy in their relationship with God. He is there and so are they and access to Him is fully granted. Your loved ones are in His presence as we speak, enjoying the matchless privileges of communion.

7. Those in Heaven seem to be aware of what is happening on earth given that these martyrs know that their killers have not yet been judged. They long for justice – and so will we. When we are in this intermediate state there will be no sense of ambivalence towards what is

happening on earth. Rather we will long for the justice of Jesus to fall so that He reigns supreme.

Furthermore, isn't it fascinating to see that these martyrs are praying for God's judgement to fall on those who are still hurting Christians in the world. They are interceding for the suffering church which suggests, as Alcorn says, 'that saints in Heaven are both seeing and praying for saints on Earth.'[3] The family of God who are already in Heaven have a deeply affectionate bond with the family of God on earth. They are their 'fellow servants, brothers and sisters.'

8. The phrase 'wait a little longer' tells us that those who are in this Heaven are still longing for a time when Jesus reigns and there is no more sin. This will not be the case in the New Heavens and New Earth but it will be the case should we die before Christ returns. We will yearn in this Heaven for the eternal Heaven. This also teaches us that we will be aware of the passing of time in Heaven.

There is much we do not know of the future but this is surely a beautiful glimpse of the goodness to come. The intermediate Heaven and the Heaven we will dwell in after Christ comes are not the same. As we wait on the latter we will be in the presence of God and yet fully conscious that this is not the end goal of our salvation. There is yet more to come. More wonder and joy to savour in another home which will one day be ours.

However frail you feel today, and however far Heaven seems from your grasp, would you remember that you 'have' eternal life (1 John 5:13). It will never be snatched from your grasp. The life that Jesus offers has begun and it will lead us through this world, the intermediate world, and on into the new world where only goodness reigns.

---

3 Ibid.

Chapter Twelve

The Way that leads to Redemption

'And the One seated on the throne said, "Behold, I make all things new." Then He said to me, "Write this down, for these words are true and faithful."'

Revelation 21:5

All that is good in this world is tainted and spoiled to some degree, and I don't think you need me to tell you that. Wherever you are today, and no matter if it includes a beach and a deckchair, there will always be a sense that life here hasn't delivered. We have come to accept that holidays end, health declines, relationships get spoiled and excitement wanes. This is part of life in a flawed world. Having just returned from a family holiday on Scotland's west coast, I know these feelings only too well. It was magnificent, but it is now over, and the toil of work is ahead.

We have already observed that when a Christian dies they enter a transitional phase that sits between the world we leave and the world we are going to. In short, we will not yet be in our forever home. We will know much goodness in this intermediate heaven but, with appetites piqued, we will long with all of our beings for the day of the Lord when Christ returns to bring an end to history. It is only then that the door to the eternal Heaven will open. Christ Himself will beckon us to enter and together with every single saint from all of time we will breathe the air of our new home.

Since Eden's ruin there has been a nostalgia in our hearts for what once was. We naturally wonder what Adam and Eve experienced in the perfection of a stunning earth that knew nothing of the consequences of sin. Every relationship was unsullied. Like the smell of a new car, or the pristine iPhone when it is first unboxed, so the earth was magnificently reflecting the glories of God. There was a beauty to all human interactions with each other, the environment, the animal kingdom, and crucially with God. How far we have fallen since those days. There is no comparison now. The new car smell has faded and the iPhone is cracked and barely functions. There are sparks of that lost paradise all around us but sin has clearly had its way.

It therefore goes without saying that welling up in the hearts of every child of God is a desire for a world that is new. A place that will never experience another person's demise. A perfect home that will forever be ours.

The Redemption of the Earth

It is vitally important as we think of Heaven that we accurately recall the promise of Christ in Revelation 21:5. It would be easy to lazily jumble His words and read that He has promised 'to make all new things'. If He has indeed said that, we would still be on course for a tremendously exciting future indeed. We would anticipate it and wonder what joys were in store. And yet please note that Christ has not said this. His promise is not to make all sorts of new things. Rather, He has vowed 'to make all things new.' That is a very different proposition. Essentially, Jesus is going to take all of the created order that He has made, and then restore it to the 'new' condition that it once was in. He has redemption on His heart. A member of our church is restoring an old Model T Ford until the insides and outsides are in straight-off-the-assembly-line condition. The old is being renovated and this is what Christ has vowed with a whole Universe that needs to be bought back from the curse it is under. Our Lord went to the cross in order to restore everything that is broken and brand new condition is the quality He seeks.

To be honest, for years of my Christian life I was sure that God's intention was to destroy our current world and start all over with a brand new design. As if it all was doomed and Heaven would not look anything like down here. It has only been in the last number of years that my eyes have been opened to the wider plot line of the Scriptures where God is intent, not on trashing the earth and discarding it to the rubbish heap, but on renewing it.

Listen to Peter: 'Heaven must receive him (Christ) until the time comes for God to **restore everything**, as he promised long ago through his holy prophets.' (Acts 3:21)

Or listen to Jesus: 'Truly I tell you, **at the renewal of all things**, when the Son of Man sits on his glorious throne, you who have followed me will also sit on twelve thrones, judging the twelve tribes of Israel.' (Matt. 19:28)

This is not a Christ who is creating a whole bunch of new things but rather, a Christ who is taking existing things and bringing renewal. In fact, even in all the miracles of Jesus (except one where the fig tree is cursed) there is a desire in all that He does to fix the broken. He is found to be rolling back the effects of sin as He renews sight, life, and calm on the lake. Leprosy is banished and demons expelled. Jesus in His ministry was revealing the heart of God, not to rubbish what He had made but to repair.

What this means is this: when we ask the question out of our longing hearts if Eden will be restored, the answer is an unequivocal *yes*. And if we are struggling to imagine what this new world might look like then I would encourage you to open your eyes. Don't close them and dream. Open them and look. This world is our reference point when we think of the world to come. When you catch a stunning sunset, imagine how beautiful it will be in a flawless world. When you experience the joy of relationships, imagine how fulfilling they will be in a sinless world. A world without disease, decay, or any decline.

The term 'Heaven and Earth' is the way that Scriptures speak of the Universe as a whole. Therefore, when Revelation 21:1 points to 'a new heaven and a new earth' we should anticipate that every molecule is going to pass through the restorative hands of our Lord. Nothing will be left untouched. The mountains, trees, valleys, stars, animals and all in-between are going to experience how it feels to be made new by the original designer. They will still be what they were made to be but just superior. Moreover, as the word 'new' (*kainos*) is used of the 'new' heavens and earth, so it is also used of a believer, 'a new creation' in 2 Corinthians 5:17. This is helpful because Christians are still the same people they once were. I am still Graham. I am still the son of John and Jan. It's just that on Aug 21st, 1983 I became a 'new' (*kainos*) creation. I have been transformed and, by grace, I am being renewed – and so it will be with our new home.

As Charles Spurgeon once noted:

> An old theologian once said, "Who chides a servant for taking away the first course when the second course consists of far greater delicacies?" Who then can regret that this present world passes away when he sees that an eternal world of joy is coming.[1]

Will we be capable of sinning in Heaven?

Sinlessness! Is this not one of the greatest desires that we have as children of God? I am tired of my imperfections. I know those around me are too. I can sense that the Spirit is making progress as year succeeds year but, while far from who I once was I am very far from who I want to be. There are evenings when, as a dad, I fall into bed at the end of a difficult day and wish I had handled multiple situations with our children in a more Christ-like manner. I am still more critical of the flaws in them than I am of my own. Indeed, if the greatest commandment is to 'love the Lord your God with all of your heart' (Matt. 22:37) then I know I still have deep issues with my heart.

Therefore, please remember this joy that is ahead for us all. In Heaven we will be stripped of any capacity to sin against our God. The reason for this is clear. The work of Christ who has died in our place has not only bought your pardon but also your freedom. The power of sin in your life is broken and so your days of failure are very limited indeed. In this world you are still going to angrily

---

1 Sorenson, S. *The Best of Charles Spurgeon* (Honor Books, 2005), 505.

bang cupboards and struggle with lust, even while the Spirit sanctifies you. You will still have parental regrets and times when your heart cools towards your Saviour. This is the spiritual battle that remains as we stay in the flesh. But not in the next world. Not then! Not when you are raised bearing the righteousness of Christ. This is what Jesus has paid for. He died, according to Hebrews 9:26, in order 'to do away with sin'. Isn't that a wonderful expression? Christ went through the sufferings of the cross in order to do away with evil, and so in the eternal Heaven there will be no place at all for sin. It will be gone for good. Like cancer being eradicated from a body, so will sin be eradicated from our hearts. Not even a trace of it will be left.

Additionally, everyone else who is there will also be in the same brand new condition as you. They will relate to you perfectly, and you to them. Your tone as you speak, your desires, and even your worship of God will be precisely as it should be. I love the way Paul Helm has referenced this for us. He says:

> The freedom of heaven, then, is the freedom from sin; not that the believer just happens to be free from sin, but that he is so constituted or reconstituted that he cannot sin. He doesn't want to sin, and he doesn't want to want sin.[2]

In the new heavens and earth there will be no temptation to be faced, for what could possibly tempt us as we live surrounded with only goodness. Satan will not be there. Only God! In His home He sets the rules, and His rule is that purity reigns. Furthermore, every time we look

2 Helm, P. *The Last Things* (Banner of Truth, 1989), 81.

at Christ and see the cost of our sin in His nail-scarred hands, we will remember that sin is ugly. Down here in this world I can be enticed, but not when I get there. Here, I can't even begin to imagine how a holy God views my sin, but in Heaven I will know. I will actually be as perfect as He is and sin will no longer pull me or have any hold. Only God and His ways will be right to me, and everything else repugnant..

Will we be capable of suffering in Heaven?

There is a young man called Jonny who attends our church. He is significantly handicapped, both mentally and physically. I adore him and every time he interrupts my preaching with his noises it gladdens my heart. He has wonderful parents who have afforded him the best care possible but his life in this world has been impaired. There are limits to what he can do. Many of the experiences that his peers have enjoyed have bypassed him. One of the joys of the gospel is anticipating what Jonny has before him. The very second he exits this world and goes into the intermediate Heaven he will be free from the curbs that his health have brought. Much the same as the sufferings of the thief of the cross which ended with his last breath, so Jonny will forever be released.

However, as good as this is, a greater joy for Jonny will be when he is called by Christ into the eternal Heaven. The resurrection of his earthly body will have taken place and made fit for Heaven, and it will be given to Jonny forever. I can't even begin to comprehend what this will be like for him. I can't even begin to comprehend what it will be like for me to see him. His wheelchair will be gone and off he will set to explore and enjoy. With wide-eyed amazement he will worship Jesus for this gift that Calvary purchased.

Of course, this will be the same experience for every saint on that day. Think of someone who is deaf being able to hear the noise of the new creation. Or picture someone who has been blind from birth being able to look through renewed eyes at the face of their Lord. We all are suffering to some degree. We are definitely all decaying. In Heaven 'He will wipe every tear from their eyes. There will be no more death or mourning or crying or pain.' (Rev. 21:4).

We mentioned Joni Eareckson Tada earlier. Her life in this world was forever changed by her diving accident aged 17. Her story of faith in the midst of her own journey of suffering has enabled countless Christians to keep going. She writes:

> I still can hardly believe it. I, with shrivelled, bent fingers, atrophied muscles, gnarled knees, and no feeling from the shoulder down, will one day have a new body, light, bright and clothed in righteousness – powerful and dazzling. Can you imagine the hope this gives someone spinal-cord injured like me? Or someone who is cerebral-palsied, brain-injured, or who has multiple sclerosis? Imagine the hope this gives someone who is manic-depressive. No other religion, no other philosophy promises new bodies, hearts and minds. Only in the gospel of Christ do hurting people find such incredible hope.'

Is this not wonderful to you? And doesn't it spur you on, no matter what condition you are in today? To be clear, I am in no way trying to diminish your suffering. This world is sore and being trapped in a body that is not functioning as it should is a deep experience that requires much grace. But be encouraged, friend. Your Heavenly Father has great things in store for you. I am certain that one of our greatest joys when we make it to the new world will be watching joy unfold in others. To see Jonny or Joni or those that are dear to us experience freedom from pain will cause us to worship our Saviour all the more. We will share in their freedom as we experience our own.

There are some who are concerned that Heaven will in some way be boring, but I want to assure you that it is going to exceed our wildest imaginations. A restored creation will be ours to enjoy endlessly. I hope you are saying, 'Graham, I can't wait!' Furthermore, we will share it as one family. Our relationships with one another, while different, will be perfected and wonderfully intimate. We will spend our lives with those whom we loved in this world, as well as those whom we never got to meet before Heaven. Reunions will be so sweet. Augustine said once:

> We have not lost our dear ones who have departed from this life, but have merely sent them ahead of us, so we also shall depart and shall come to that life where they will be more than ever dear as they will be better known to us, and where we shall love them without fear of parting.[3]

Old relationships restored. New relationships begun. And all in a place from which sin and suffering are forever displaced. I find myself excited and savouring the future. This world truly is not my resting place. This is why Adoniram Judson once exclaimed:

---

3 Augustine. *The City of God* (Penguin, 2003), 22:19, 2; 22:20, 3 (301).

When Christ calls me home I shall go with the gladness of a boy bounding away from school.[4]

4 Vance, C. *Adoniram Judson: Devoted for Life* (Christian Focus, 2013), 539.

Chapter Thirteen

The Way that leads to God

‘One thing I ask from the Lord, this only do I seek: that I may dwell in the house of the Lord
all the days of my life, to gaze on the beauty of the Lord and to seek him in his temple.’

Psalm 27:4

It seems wrong in a sense to have left it until the very end of this book to address the most soul-satisfying blessing that Heaven will provide. If we were to grade what it is that the Christian needs most, then surely we would have plunged into this theme at the start. However, having established what kind of Heaven we will inhabit, we come now to think of what company we will keep. Ultimately, this is where The Way is taking us – the eternal privilege of being with God and beholding Him. This arduous journey that we are on is not simply leading us to a better new world that will be shared with Christians. That in itself would be a wonderful reality, but there is much more, and our calling to come home is much higher. In the end, whether we leave this world in death or at the Lord’s return, we will open our eyes and see the face of God.

What we must learn as we grow in grace is that God is not wanting your affection for His blessings to supersede your affection for Him. That of course would be idolatry. We may be excited (and rightly so) about being in Heaven with loved ones. Your Heavenly Father doesn't just understand that. He wants that. Being reunited with those we have lost is a blessing that Christ suffered to purchase. However, please understand that your deepest joy is not going to be found in seeing your mother again. It will be found in seeing God and discovering more of Him for all eternity.

A Unified Heaven and Earth

We have already observed that the term 'heaven and earth' is the way that the Scriptures speak of the entirety of the Universe. Heaven is the home of God and His angels. Earth is the home of all He has made. As we live in the here and now these two worlds are not joined and a gulf exists between them. But, in the new creation there will be nothing separating the two. Belinda Carlisle was onto something when she released her 1987 hit single, 'Heaven is a Place on Earth.' The truth of what she was singing about was clearly lost on her, for in Biblical terms that will be the reality we enjoy. Heaven will be on earth. God will make His home among us. To use the words of Rev. 21:3, 'God Himself will be with them.' As Randy Alcorn points out, 'going to Heaven without God would be like a bride going on her honeymoon without her groom.'[1]

It is this great hope of seeing God that has propelled millions of saints onwards on The Way. This world is distracting. When you sit down for devotions I am sure

1 Alcorn, R. *Heaven* (Tyndale House, 2004), 55.

your mind will often wander away. There will be days in your journey when you are not gripped with thoughts of God. You will enjoy the company of others much more for they can be touched and seen. God will seem distant to you. The invisible will seem intangible and you will need to fight for the intimacy that you need as a believer. While not excusing this for a second I do want to acknowledge that this is the spiritual conflict that every Christian faces. You are not alone and you are not strange. It is possible to be near to God in this world. It is even possible to see Him, for Paul discloses that His invisible qualities are on display all around us in creation (Rom. 1:20). However, when the moment comes for you to open your eyes in Heaven itself, be assured that God's presence and glory will be on full display. You will never find Him boring and you will never have had enough. As Jonathan Edwards said,

> To go to heaven fully to enjoy God, is infinitely better than the most pleasant accommodations here. Fathers and mothers, husbands, wives, children, or the company of earthly friends, are but shadows. But the enjoyment of God is the substance. These are the scattered beams, but God is the sun. These are the streams, but God is the fountain. These are but drops, but God is the ocean.[2]

To be clear, I don't think we can be definitive about what seeing God, who is Spirit, will mean. Will we see Him physically? I think we will have to wait to find out. One thing is absolutely sure and that is that we will see Jesus. Or as Paul would succinctly state it, to be away from the

---

2 Edwards, J. 'The Christian Pilgrim', sermon preached in 1733, quoted in Alistair E. McGrath, *A Brief History of Heaven* (Blackwell, 2003), 575.

body is 'to be at home with the Lord' (2 Cor. 5:8). In this life we often feel the shame of letting our Saviour down. We still fail as Christians. Every week a silence overcomes us when we ought to speak for Him and share His gospel. But in the New World we will never disappoint Him, and we will never feel shame. We will stand perfected. We will be thoroughly renewed...and we will love Him with all of our beings. Our worship will flow. He will be our greatest pleasure. I must be honest with you. I find it both astonishing and exciting to know that not too long from now I am going to be able to look on the face of Christ. Do you not feel the same? Being able to walk with Jesus and sing, climb, explore, discover, laugh and eat with our Saviour. The disciples knew this for a few short years but they were still in their fallen flesh. In Heaven it will be forever, and we will be in our glorified bodies.

Dear friends, this is where The Way is taking us all. Unfettered worship is coming. I truly believe that Heaven will be spent discovering more of our God. More of His wonders. More of His might. More of His beautiful character. And the more we discover, the more we will sing. Perhaps it will be that you will make a friend in Heaven. Someone whose life in this world had no merits. They will tell you their story and how it was they were drawn into the Kingdom. You will then share your own story and how it was that, filled with flaws, regrets and shame you encountered grace that was truly amazing. I anticipate that this will happen again and again. The sharing of stories in the presence of Father, Son and Holy Spirit whose glories shine like the sun. And in the end we will all be saying, 'and to think that *this* God would shower His love on me.'

I am not saying that we will always be prostrate on our knees before our Lord for all time. That would be to ignore all of the other activities to which Scripture points to, such as meals where we eat and drink, times when we work for our God, walking etc. Clearly we will not always be lying on the ground. Rather, and this is crucial – whatever we do will be an act of worship. An act of perfect worship. Should we walk somewhere, or talk to a friend, or eat a meal in the company of the Apostle Paul, we will do it with Christ as our greatest treasure. Not for one second will He be replaced or ignored. Perhaps it will be that on the occasions when we gather with others the volume of praise will rise but, in Heaven we will fulfil 1 Thessalonians 5:16 to the letter – we will 'be joyful always.' There will be a spontaneity that won't require the church structures which we currently need in this world. Here we really did need our Lord to institute a meal of bread and wine so that we 'remembered' and didn't forget. But in Heaven there will be no need for Sunday morning services or Wednesday night Bible studies that call us to worship. Rather, we will be in a state of worship all the time. We were made to worship and we will be remade to worship.

I have a friend whose company is always exhilarating. His conversation is always packed full of anecdotes that make my life look as dull as dishwater. Being around him is fun. I always look forward to the times we share and enjoy learning more of what has been happening in his life. If this is how I feel sharing a coffee with a deeply sinful friend, can you even begin to picture our fascination with Jesus Christ when we are perfected. Won't we be riveted? We recently attended a wedding where the groom just could not take his eyes off his new bride. She was dazzling to him and he looked like the cat that had got the cream. This, in full measure, is what is coming for you. You will look on your Lord and love Him with such intensity, and that love will continue to pulsate in you at the optimum level that is possible for a perfected human being. It will never abate. Here we wish we could love Him more, but there we will love Him more and more.

I love how J.I. Packer pictures this. He says:

> Hearts on earth may say in the course of a joyful experience, "I don't want this ever to end." But invariably it does. The hearts of those in Heaven say, "I want this to go on forever." And it will. There is no better news than this.[3]

How to think in the light of Heaven

When Paul wrote to the church in Colossae he told them to 'set your minds on things above, not on earthly things.' (Col. 3:2) With this in mind, given our minds often struggle to follow this instruction, here are some thoughts that will help us to live well in the light of the coming reward.

- Life is merely a vapour (James 4:14). It really is over in the blink of an eye. My time here in this world is so short in comparison to the quantity of time that awaits. Live for the things that last. That dream home or that lifestyle will soon be left. It would be foolish in the extreme to put down roots in a world or life that is passing away. 'Storing up for yourselves treasures on earth' is to live for things that moths eat.

3 Packer, J. I. *Concise Theology* (InterVarsity Press, 1993), 266.

- Heaven is real. If you have Christ you will go there and be as conscious as you are in this world. It will be physical. Something you can touch with your hands. You will smell it and hear it. A place you will deeply enjoy. Meditate on it.

- Every single person you meet today will ultimately end up in either Heaven or Hell. Your priority, aside from getting there yourself, is to take as many others with you as you can. Share the gospel. Tell them that Jesus wishes to invite them to The Way.

- Suffering here is real but it is not lasting. One day it will be a footnote in your experience. Hang in there and hang on. The Lord is going to redeem that body of yours and make it fit for a new world. It will be flawless. The greatest times in your experience are all before you.

- You are going to be in the presence of your Heavenly Father and you are going to see your risen Lord Jesus. Set your mind on that.

- Heaven will not be boring. It will feel like your best ever day that lasts forever. Nothing will impede your happiness. Nothing will ever disappoint.

- In the same way that God looked at creation in Genesis and said it was 'good', so you will only know goodness in the New Creation.

- Heaven will be full of rewards for those who have lived for Christ in this world. We will get there purely because of grace, but when we get there we will discover that how we lived here really mattered. Therefore, live every day with one eye on Heaven (Rom. 2:6).

Conclusion

I was a young boy when I became a Christian. I'm not sure I understood fully what I was getting into at the time. I only knew that Jesus had died for my sins and that I needed a Saviour who could forgive and redeem. The spiritual conflict ahead was obscured to me in large measure. It was a simplistic beginning, but it was real. My destination had altered and life would never be the same again.

Much time has elapsed since then and I am so thankful He has kept me. Many mistakes have been made and many regrets pepper my past. My journey to Heaven so far has not been a straight line. It feels like it has been so long and at times it has felt arduous. I have had times when I have wondered if I will make it. And yet Jesus is faithful. Of course He is. He is for the weary ones. He is committed to the flaky. He will finish His work in me and I know He will lead me home.

Can I encourage you as you prepare to set this book on a shelf somewhere to invest in healthy spiritual relationships. Every journey is better when others are there, and this journey is no different. Learn to confide. That is, learn to share your struggles and walk with others. I'm not encouraging you to unzip yourself to everyone and let all of your secrets come tumbling out. However, finding companions you can trust and making yourself vulnerable with them is integral to this relational journey. Perhaps a band of brothers or sisters in your church who are committed to going deeper with the Lord? Or perhaps meeting frequently with someone to study? Definitely in your marriage. If I can suggest an essential for your tool kit as you keep going, it would be that you reject solo Christianity and you gather around you trusted travellers.

Do you remember how this is beautifully expressed in Psalm 122:1? 'I rejoiced with those who said to me, let us go to the house of the Lord.' Here is a worshipper who has great friends. 'Let's go', they said. 'Let's get to God's house. We're going, and so are you.' I need these relationships and so do you. And in the end my song (and my friends' song) will be the same,

All the way my Saviour leads me–
Oh, the fullness of His love!
Perfect rest to me is promised
In my Father's house above.
When my spirit, clothed immortal,
Wings its flight to realms of day,
This my song through endless ages:
Jesus led me all *the way*;
This my song through endless ages:
Jesus led me all *the way.*[1]

1 Fanny Crosby, 1875.

Also available from Christian Focus ...

978-1-5271-0893-6

Growing in Christ

5 Biblical Steps for Enduring Growth

Paul Wells

What does it mean to 'grow in the grace and knowledge of our Lord and Saviour Jesus Christ'? In this valuable book, Paul Wells takes the reader through the five conditions favourable for growth in Christ: planting in the right place for spiritual life to begin; rooting in the biblical teaching of the word of God; growing up to stability in Christ; maturity and vitality through the work of the Spirit; and fruitfulness as the outcome of growth into Christ.

Includes discussion questions at the end of each chapter.

... a succinct, helpful, biblical, theological, and practical book that details enduring growth through five biblical steps ... By the Spirit's grace, this book will instruct, edify, and mature you in our wonderful Saviour, so that you will bear fruit to His glory.

Joel R. Beeke

Chancellor, Puritan Reformed Theological Seminary, Grand Rapids, Michigan

Zack Eswine

WISER *with* JESUS

Overcoming the Temptations that Hinder Your Relationships, Steal Your Time, Mar Your Decision-Making and Thwart Your Purpose

978-1-5271-1223-0

Wiser with Jesus

Overcoming the Temptations that Hinder Your Relationships, Steal Your Time, Mar Your Decision-Making and Thwart Your Purpose

Zack Eswine

Dive into the godly wisdom of Proverbs with Zack Eswine's guide to living well.

The biblical book of Proverbs exemplifies how to live life on this earth in the best way possible. However, rather than giving us step–by–step instructions on how to live a more efficient, productive, and successful life, the ancient book of Proverbs encourages us to meditate on the person, posture and pace of wisdom.

In this valuable book, Zack Eswine shows us how these things play out in our everyday lives. He emphasizes the importance of relating wisely to people, including to ourselves, before considering how to grow wiser in life skills. But to grow wiser of heart, whether with people or with life skills, wisdom invites us to prayer and community. Biblical wisdom invites us to seek wiser hearts in communal rather than lonely ways.

Christian Focus Publications

Our mission statement

Staying Faithful

In dependence upon God we seek to impact the world through literature faithful to His infallible Word, the Bible. Our aim is to ensure that the Lord Jesus Christ is presented as the only hope to obtain forgiveness of sin, live a useful life and look forward to heaven with Him.

Our Books are published in four imprints:

CHRISTIAN FOCUS

Popular works including biographies, commentaries, basic doctrine and Christian living.

MENTOR

Books written at a level suitable for Bible College and seminary students, pastors, and other serious readers. The imprint includes commentaries, doctrinal studies, examination of current issues and church history.

CHRISTIAN HERITAGE

Books representing some of the best material from the rich heritage of the church.

CF4KIDS

Children's books for quality Bible teaching and for all age groups: Sunday school curriculum, puzzle and activity books; personal and family devotional titles, biographies and inspirational stories – because you are never too young to know Jesus!

Christian Focus Publications Ltd,
Geanies House, Fearn, Ross-shire,
IV20 1TW, Scotland, United Kingdom.
www.christianfocus.com